# Golden Jubilee

## The Federal Land Distribution Act and The Unexecuted Supreme Court Order

DAVe MyeR is A LONGTIME
FRieND AND I AM HONOReD
He HAS SHAReD GolDeN Jubilee
WITH you! I Hope you
ENJoy THe ReAD!

RICH GOLDEN

RICH
GOLDeN

NEWMAN SPRINGS PUBLISHING
320 Broad Street
Red Bank, NJ 07701

First originally published by Newman Springs Publishing 2021

ISBN 978-1-63692-779-4 (Paperback)
ISBN 978-1-63692-780-0 (Digital)

Printed in the United States of America

# Contents

# Introduction

In 1986, I began a detailed research related to Jubilee. Fourteen years later, in the year 2000, I copyrighted my first book, submitted copies to publishers across the nation, and traveled to publishing seminars in various cities without success. However, the book was ahead of its time and contained controversial information regarding high-profile leaders from across this nation. It was considered too hot for anyone to touch, or perhaps it was divine providence. There were no takers, and self-publishing and e-books were not yet common in the industry, so I bought up all the copies and put them on the shelf. Fast-forward twenty years later, and the book reveals numerous predictions that have come true, including the following:

I predicted Hillary Clinton would lose her presidential bid for the White House even though everyone expected her to win. I predicted she would lose the election to a Washington outsider, a billionaire businessman with a loudmouth and a propensity for the unexpected. That is exactly what happened when Donald Trump won the 2016 election and became president of the United States.

I predicted this new president would restructure the privately owned and unconstitutional Federal Reserve

Bank. That is exactly what President Trump is doing, as he has now moved the Federal Reserve under the authority of the Treasury Department, which he officially oversees.

I predicted the IRS would be completely restructured. Currently, reforming the IRS to a simple sales tax plan, along with the elimination of payroll taxes altogether, is being discussed in Washington.

I predicted there would be a massive unexplained surplus of trillions of dollars discovered in the Federal Reserve. We are currently witnessing the distribution of these funds to the American citizenry in the form of stimulus checks. The mainstream media is unable to explain the source of these funds. However, twenty years ago, this surplus was disclosed by yours truly and will be discussed in detail in later chapters of this book.

Twenty years ago, I predicted a national and subsequent global Jubilee, or forgiveness of debt. Today, Jubilee is commonly discussed among nations, as details of a global reset in the form of debt forgiveness are being considered.

I also predicted, along with the disclosure of these unexplained trillions of dollars discovered in the Federal Reserve, a plan to distribute the wealth hidden in federal and state lands to the American people. That plan is revealed in this book as well, along with how it will positively affect the major problems in society today.

The fact that these predictions are currently coming true in front of our eyes, given thirty-five years of detailed research on the subject of Jubilee and how it relates to our nation in modern times, would constitute me to be a credible witness in any court of law on the subject of

Jubilee. To be clear, I have no degrees hanging on my wall. I have a high school diploma and two years of college, and a seminary degree from Cornerstone Bible Institute. But at an early age, I found my calling, and it is revealed in the following pages to the benefit of every American citizen, regardless of age, race, gender, sexual orientation, and/or religious background.

This is the beauty of the Jubilee Land Plan—all are treated equal, no matter who you are, just as God's grace is given freely to all mankind equally. The reader is challenged to keep an open mind, and the sound logic contained therein will become evident; arguments against the Jubilee Land Plan will become hard to find. An explosion of light and virtual wealth for every American citizen will soon be realized, as this nation experiences a revolutionary paradigm change.

Thank you for taking the time to read *Golden Jubilee*. It is certainly my hope that you find it both interesting and inspirational!

# What Is Jubilee?

In the Old Testament, God instructed his people to enact certain principles every fifty years to rejuvenate their economy both economically and spiritually. Among the many benefits were that all lands were to be returned to their original owners, and all debts were to be forgiven. These spiritual principles formed a rebirth for the economy and for the spiritual state of the nation.

Jubilee was a symbol of freedom for the people containing many levels of spiritual, physical, and economic rejuvenation. Jubilee was also a symbol of God's unconditional love for his people, offering a clean slate and new beginning for everyone to experience at one point or another in their lifetime. There are many details in the Old Testament concerning Jubilee, which I will refrain from delving into, but the main point of emphasis is a fresh start for all.

The word *jubilee* refers to a trumpet or shout that indicates the beginning or release of the event itself. Interestingly, according to the Hebrew calendar, the official year of Jubilee was 2017, which ushered in the beginning of the Trump presidency. The official year of Jubilee, which began with a trumpet or shout, was also the beginning of the Jubilee presidency, under which the Jubilee land plan will become a reality and provide a spiritual and economic fresh start for all.

When it comes to God's prophetic timetable, there are no coincidences. It was no mistake the beginning of the great end-time Jubilee era was marked by the beginning of the Trump presidency along with a great trumpet or shout, which matched exactly the timeline of the Hebrew calendar! This book will explain the release of a modern-time Jubilee, the return of lands to the original owners, and the forgiveness of debt. Also illustrated herein are the numerous social benefits to this plan as millions of voting American citizens step into a new realm of financial liberty.

# Federal Lands Ownership

According to Wikipedia, federal lands are lands in the United States owned by the federal government. Who is the federal government? You and me, and all the citizens of the United States. We the people, of the people, for the people, and by the people. They are held in public trust and managed by the federal government. Let me repeat for the sake of the entire premise of this book.

Federal lands are lands in the United States owned by the citizens of the United States. Let us explore this concept in more detail. If federal lands are owned by the citizens of the United States, to what form of ownership does this statement refer? Other than taking a family vacation to Old Faithful, the National Seashore, or any number of federal parks from Alaska to Florida and all points in between, how exactly do the citizens own the federal land? The answer is: that is as far as their ownership goes. If the American citizens own it, should they not be able to grow their wealth in some way or sell and manage their assets in a tangible fashion if they choose? The following pages will describe a revolutionary plan to bring to life ownership of federal land by the American citizenry while leaving these federal lands pristine, untouched, and unchanged in any way.

State and county lands also fall into the same category of ownership by the American citizenry. To get the full scope of this concept, take a step back and view everything included in the categories of federal-, state-, and county-held public lands. We are not just talking about the Denali National Park in Alaska. Of course, that is a major acreage of land owned by the American citizenry, but we are also talking about all the military bases in the United States. Up and down the coastline of America, prime real estate was secured for military bases to protect our great nation. The land upon which these military bases are located is also owned by the American citizenry. The great prime oceanfront real estate of military bases and protected lands are owned by the American citizenry. The prime real estate upon which the federal buildings reside in Manhattan is owned by the American citizenry. The state and federal buildings all over our nation are also owned by the American citizenry. State parks across every state of our great nation are some of the most prime pieces of real estate in the country. There is no federal entity nor any state entity that is not fully constituted by the American citizenry.

Additionally, most American owned buildings on foreign land are owned by the American citizenry. Some buildings on foreign land are leased by American government entities; these are not owned by the American citizenry. However, to get the full scope of all lands and the buildings across the globe, those lands and buildings which fall into the category of federally owned are included in the formula by which the Jubilee Land Plan is calculated.

Like the multitude of individual pixels which make up the fine details of a photograph, every American citizen is equally represented in the ownership of land by the American citizenry, as millions of pixels put together to form a whole image. Consider the Jubilee Land Plan as similar to an oil well placed on top of a section of land. The oil well extracts the value from the land for the owner of that specific plot of land. The Jubilee Land Plan operates in a similar fashion; however, the land remains unchanged. The park rangers still maintain their job and professional responsibilities as before. The value is distributed to each American citizen in a matrix, much like the matrix used on Wall Street, which will be explained in more detail shortly. A plan of the people by the people and for the people. No longer are these just words but virtual value distributed equally to the American people, giving everyone a fresh start, which is Jubilee at its core.

# The Virtual Wealth Matrix

According to *Wikipedia*, there are 950 million acres of land owned by federal and state governments, military branches, Army Corps of Engineers, and tribal lands in the United States. Additionally, Native American tribes will continue to retain ownership of their lands but will also participate in the Jubilee Matrix. This includes all federal and state buildings in every city in America, every military base from Pearl Harbor Naval Base to Pensacola Naval Air Station; Eglin Air Force Base in Florida to Edwards Air Force Base in California; the underground military complex of NORAD in Colorado to Area 51 in Nevada; Fort Benning Army base in Georgia to the West Point Military Academy in New York; the White House, the US Capitol building and every state capitol in America; all state, federal, and local correctional facilities and hospitals; the lands upon which federal interstates run; all state-owned universities and the land upon which they are located, from Yellowstone to Yosemite; the nuclear missile silos in North Dakota to the mysterious HARRP complex in Alaska; from the Trident Submarine base in Bangor Maine to the submarine base in Mayport Florida outside of Jacksonville. Every single acre of land is accounted for in the Jubilee Matrix.

The average value per acre is determined by taking the highest value per acre of government-owned land and the lowest value per acre of government-owned land and simply dividing it by two. The high-end values of San Diego Naval Base and the Federal Building in Chicago, for example, offset the low-end value of the missile silos in North Dakota. To be completely thorough and transparent, the value of mineral rights of undeveloped lands will be included in establishing the value per acre, as the American citizenry owns the land.

That value per acre is multiplied by the total amount of acres. That gross number is then divided by the total number of American citizens registered to vote. The sum from that equation is the total value due to every voting American citizen, who will have an account with a personal code and debit card by which these extracted virtual funds will be loaded. This subject is currently being discussed regarding the future dispensation of stimulus funds to the American citizenry, and the same accounts could be used for the Jubilee Land Plan. This also would solve the problem of voter fraud as each voting citizen has their own account in the matrix with the highest levels of virtual security.

Think of the matrix used for the New York Stock Exchange. At the end of each day, there is a value determined for the marketplace because of specific values for stocks traded. The Wall Street matrix is a living, breathing entity. The matrix itself will be designed by individuals with scientific and mathematical backgrounds to create the algorithms used to process the data for the initial setup and for the continual daily operations of the matrix. Once the initial matrix distributions are made, the average value per acre of commercial and private land throughout the nation would be calculated daily. The percentage up or down from the previous day would be applied to the matrix, and a value per acre would be determined at the end of each day as well. Thus, the Jubilee Matrix would be measured as up or down a certain percentage each day. Thereby the portfolio of citizens matrix account would increase in value or decrease in value proportionately, just as Wall Street.

Every citizen would have the option to hold on to the funds in their account or cash out at any time. When they cash out, the shares would go back into the matrix. Others may choose to acquire more virtual shares in the matrix, just as a stock trader would. Again, the value per acre is determined at the end of the day, based on the information and algorithms processed throughout each day. Just as with Wall Street, the activity in the real estate market will fluctuate. Some days, the value per acre might be more than the original disbursement, and of course, it is possible that some days the market price may go down.

When an individual turns eighteen and becomes registered as a voting American citizen, they are issued the same initial disbursement into their account as was dispersed to all citizens initially. When an individual becomes deceased, their funds are returned to the matrix. This important feature maintains the integrity of the plan and prohibits individuals from acquiring massive units of wealth from the virtual matrix and handing it down to their successors when they become deceased, thereby eliminating the possibility of the wealthy manipulating the matrix in their favor. However, if a savvy businessman acquires many units from the matrix to increase the value of their portfolio, at any point in their life, they may cash out, return the shares they have acquired to the matrix, and pass their cash-out to their next generation of the family. The wealth they have acquired and returned to the matrix will offset the wealth dispersed to the American citizens who have just turned eighteen and received their disbursement from the matrix initially.

These daily activities are examples of transactions which all determine the value per share in the matrix, just as with Wall Street. Individuals can monitor the matrix daily and choose when to buy, sell, or use those funds for their own personal needs. Whatever is left in their account when they become deceased will be returned to the matrix, which, again, is a virtual breathing entity. The Federal Reserve would act as the centerpiece, logistically, for the Jubilee Matrix. More on that later.

For example: 950 million total acres in the matrix with the value of land per acre varying from $2,000 an acre to $200,000 an acre, creating a starting point of $101,000 per acre, multiplied by 950 million acres equals a total value of $95,950,000,000,000. This number divided by 200 million registered voting American citizens equals a starting point of $479,000 per voting citizen as the initial distribution in the Jubilee matrix.

Kim Clement, the late great prophet, on February 22, 2014, predicted the election of Donald Trump to the Oval Office, predicted the unsuccessful efforts to impeach him, along with a "new kind of war started against the United States by the nation of China." He then said, "a new Snowden will come along, and both Democrats and Republicans will be very afraid, saying, 'We have nowhere to hide!'" He then asks the question, "How do we kill the giant of debt?" He said,

> Take these remarks and make note of them for they are gems—the name Gold and the word *gold*. Remember that. These that reject him (Trump) shall be shocked at how he takes the giant down. Look not to Wall Street; However, observe (a hidden reference to the Jubilee Matrix). They shall ask, "What is your plan for this giant?" And he will take a simple stone—remember the name, Gold—and he shall hold it up, and they will laugh at him. But the plan is so brilliant, says the Lord, that it could only have been given by me!

In 1986, I was meditating and praying to the Lord about spiritual and financial principles laid out in his Word, contrasted against worldly financial principles, and seeking God's plan for financial planning for his people. At that moment, deep within my spirit yet audibly to my inner man, ever so clearly, I heard the word *Jubilee*. Three times in a row, I heard "Jubilee, Jubilee, Jubilee." I felt the fear of the Lord upon this as I knew I had an encounter with the Most High. This was the beginning of my path of what would become my life's destiny, culminating in this book and the fulfillment thereof.

When I began this path, I made a commitment to the Lord that I would not tell the story without bringing glory to his name. There is no need to be concerned about a so-called conflict of separation of church and state. I am merely illustrating the inspiration for the path upon which I began to walk many years ago. I am not a religious man in the way the world thinks of religion. I seek truth only.

There is one place in the Holy Scriptures and only one place that gives the definition of religion. It is in the book of James, chapter 1, verse 27, which states, "Pure religion and undefiled before God and the Father is this, to visit the fatherless and the widows in their affliction and to remain unspotted from the world." Just as King Jesus said he came to set the captives free, the goal of the Jubilee Land Plan is to set the captives free financially as a symbol of God's grace to all, which is unmerited favor. A gift distributed equally to all, with no ability nor expectation to repay, symbolic of God's love for all men and women, carrying with it also the message that the heaven-bound train will soon be leaving the station.

While in prayer recently, I heard the still small voice inside tell me to read from the book of Joshua chapter 1, verses 1–8, one of my favorite scriptures and one that I have read many times. However, as I read verse six, the words jumped off the page at me like never before, and I felt the Holy Spirit witness in my spirit, giving me confirmation that I was indeed on the right path. The Scripture in reference said, "For unto this people shalt thou divide for an inheritance, the land." This was witnessed to me, along with the prophetic words of Kim Clement and the word *Jubilee* spoken into my spirit in 1986. All were confirmations that the path I was on was of divine origin. I would be remiss if I did not divulge the backstory of how this book came to be. Truth is a force beyond the control of mortal man.

# The Jubilee Contract

As it is with Hollywood movies and Disney fairy tales, there are good guys and bad guys. This basic concept goes as far back as when Satan was a good guy in heaven known as Lucifer or Hallel from the original Hebrew text. He was one of God's most beautiful creations and was said to have spread his wings above God's throne and led the angels in musical praise to the Most-High God. Scripture describes him as one of God's most special creations. He spread his majestic wings above God's holy throne in heaven and led the angelic host in praise to their creator.

It must have been a breathtaking sight to behold! Not only was he beautiful, but he was also anointed with musical instruments created into his actual being. He became so full of himself and intoxicated with his power that he said in his heart that he would exalt himself above God's throne. As beautiful and as powerful as he was, this was not a very smart decision, for how can creation rise up and become more powerful than its creator?

As the story goes, he was banished from heaven down to the earth and took with him one-third of the angels as well, so he must have been quite convincing. When he deceived Eve in the original garden, and Adam followed along, the earth became his dominion, as he is referred to in Scripture as the God of this world. From that point in time to the present day, his mission became singular in his attempt to lure God's creation from worshipping their creator to one of them worshipping himself. His hatred is not toward God; his hatred is toward mankind for replacing himself as God's most favored creation.

Throughout the centuries, we see a repeated pattern of Satan's influence upon kings and kingdoms of the earth. He promises the wealth of the world in exchange for the allegiance of world leaders to himself. Fast-forward to the present day, and we see this pattern continued. The battle for the soul of America is on display. Clearly a war of good versus evil. Satan knows the Bible better than most preachers, and he knows his time is short. He also knows that in the end, he does not win. However, this only makes his rage more intense.

In the fall of 2016, the laptop computer of Anthony Weiner, former United States congressman from New York, was seized in his arrest. When his laptop was audited by the authorities, there was a file discovered titled "Insurance." His wife was Huma Abedin, the right-hand assistant to Hillary Clinton. She also had brothers at the top of the leadership of the Muslim Brotherhood organization. Discovered on this laptop were mountains of information, examples of how many leaders of this nation had sold their souls and their allegiance to Satan for positions of power in this world. Some examples found on this computer were such that seasoned veterans of the New York City Police

Department became sick from watching it; they were so disgusted.

Without going into detail, this is a modern-day example of good versus evil. These dark forces never expected Hillary Clinton to lose. They did not accept the results of the election and created a series of facades to protest their rejection of the election results to the American people. First it was Russian collusion, then the unsuccessful Mueller report made up of a series of baseless accusations leading to a failed impeachment attempt of President Trump.

Throughout the first half of 2020, there have been riots in major cities across the nation based on racial inequity. These rioters have confessed to responding to ads from organizations such as Antifa and other George Soros-backed groups, offering the rioters as much as twenty-five dollars an hour to stir up as much chaos and social discord as possible, crying out to the world how awful things are in America. Just as Satan discards his followers when he has no more use for them, there are now reports that some Antifa protestors are suing George Soros for failure to pay on his promises.

My point in illustrating the good-versus-evil conflict from the origin of time to the present day is this: The Jubilee Land Plan makes many of these problems go away. When every voting American citizen receives their initial disbursement of close to one half million dollars, those in captivity financially are set free, and it is a new day of opportunity for all. There is no social injustice; there is financial freedom for all.

Those who grew up in a household with little to no money now have a future of endless opportunity. A family with two parents now can send their kids to school, start their own business, or pursue their own dreams. There is no need for one neighbor to steal from another neighbor. The opportunity for success is the same for all. The enforcer who will motivate all recipients of the Jubilee Land Plan to play by the rules is that along with each disbursement will come a contract each recipient signs prior to receiving funds in their account.

The contract simply states anyone found guilty of committing a crime, such as initiating violence and riots after signing the contract and receiving their funds, will serve an automatic ten-year jail sentence, and their Jubilee Land Plan disbursement will be returned to the matrix. This one rule is simple and nonnegotiable and will serve as motivation for all registered voting American citizens. If you are not a registered voting American citizen, I believe there is sufficient information laid out in the Jubilee Land Plan for which to become one. The funds provided in the dispensation of the Jubilee Land Plan clearly exceed any evildoer's ability to provide sufficient financial incentive to citizens to oppose the plan. Thus, America becomes Lake Placid. Truly a peaceful land of opportunity for all!

# Timing Is Everything

*Timing is everything.* Everyone has probably heard this often overused statement; perhaps it is overused because it is true. The following story illustrates how the timing of decision-making affects so many things beyond our ability to view the world and the invisible walls with which we surround ourselves.

A good friend of mine from my high school days, who I will refer to as Dave, also happened to be the son of the boss of my father, who I will refer to as Mr. Tatum. My father was Secretary and General Counsel of a privately owned corporation in Ohio owned by the Tatum family. Mr. Tatum attended Harvard University and became friends with George H. W. Bush, who attended Yale, during a series of debate competitions. Their friendship lasted over the years, and Mrs. Tatum, through her specific training in college and years of practice, became the spiritual advisor to President Bush, who consulted with her over the years on both political and spiritual matters. The Tatum family purchased a beautiful estate in Ponte Vedra, Florida, and prior to the first Gulf War in 1990, President Bush scheduled a meeting in Ponte Vedra with Mrs. Tatum to discuss his plans and strategy for the Gulf War and his reelection campaign.

My friend Dave remembered there were some baby monitors left at the house for use when his sister visited with her young twins. When he became aware of the president's pending visit, he cleverly placed one of the baby monitors in a hidden location in Mrs. Tatum's office where the counseling session would take place. He put the other one in his room. When the Secret Service agents scanned the house prior to the president's arrival, the baby monitors remained under the radar, and Dave was able to remotely spy on this mother and the president. He soon became aware of one of the most high-profile, secret political plans ever created.

Dave and I reconnected after years of going our separate ways, and soon after, I visited him at their Ponte Vedra estate. He told me the entire story with a sly grin on his face, proud of himself that he had outsmarted the Secret Service. He showed me exactly where the monitors were hidden, where the president sat, and where his mother sat, bringing the interesting tale to life while we looked over the amazing view of the Ponte Vedra coastline and the Atlantic Ocean.

Dave recalled the president outlining the details of his plan, designed to create the image of a successful wartime president riding the wave of his popularity all the way to reelection, returning home as the hero who saved the world from an evil monster. He expected his spiritual advisor, Mrs. Tatum, to agree that it was a perfect plan for reelection. After carefully listening quietly, without hesitation and with an air of confidence, she responded with an answer the president was not prepared to hear. She simply said, "Your timing is off. You are going to peak too soon. Your popularity rating will fade prior to the election instead of peaking at the election like you had planned."

And that was it; the meeting was over. The president clearly was not pleased with the answer yet remained polite and appreciative of Mrs. Tatum's time. Just as quickly as they had arrived, the Secret Service agents escorted the president into the parade of black presidential vehicles, away from the estate, and they were gone. The president was stiff-necked and rejected the counsel he sought as he did not get the answer he wanted, but he proceeded nevertheless with this plan.

History will recall the drama of seeing the Gulf War play out on TV unlike any series of events in history, ushering in a new age of modern weaponry. The war against Saddam Hussein was over almost as quickly as it started. The president's approval rating soared to over 70 percent after the war, but in the end, Mrs. Tatum's counsel to the president rang true. He did indeed peak too soon and surrendered the White House to Bill Clinton in 1992.

There are many examples in the history of the timing working for or against those who manipulate the events. Proverbs states the heart of the king is in the hand of the Lord, and as the river runs its course, he turns it whithersoever he will. This scripture illustrates how God turns the hearts of kings and presidents in the direction he chooses to affect the timing and outcome of world events. The earth is God's footstool.

A famous biblical story that illustrates the importance of timing is that of Abraham, Isaac, and Ishmael. God had promised Abraham a son, but he did not disclose when this son would be born. Many years passed, and Abraham's wife, Sarah, suggested that perhaps God meant for Abraham to take Sarah's handmaiden, Hagar, make love to her and she would bear Abraham a child. Abraham did as Sarah suggested, and soon, they had a child whom they named Ishmael.

Ishmael had become a teenager when God delivered on his promise to Abraham and Sarah gave birth to Isaac, from whom God intended to populate the promised land from Abraham's seed with a multitude of people equaling the sand in the sea. There was extreme friction between Sarah and Isaac and Hagar and Ishmael. Abraham was distressed, and his solution to the problem was to give Hagar and Ishmael water and bread and send them out into the wilderness to wander aimlessly. Certainly not an act of love to the mother of his child. When their supplies ran out, God heard their cries and had mercy on them, sending an angel to supernaturally open their eyes to a well of water. The angel told them God would make a great nation out of them and directed them to Egypt, where Ishmael found a wife and began to build his family and nation.

Because Abraham was not only disobedient to God's instruction but also misread the timing of events, the animosity between Isaac and Ishmael, which started millennia ago, exists even today between the Hebrew people and the Arab people. This is illustrated most clearly in the city of Jerusalem, where the holy Islamic temple is built upon the foundation of the Hebrew temple of David, causing one of the most imposing obstacles to peace the world has ever known, all because of timing.

My journey and the timing of this story met several roadblocks as I tried to pitch the original book. I wrote and adjusted it many times over the past two decades when I thought the political timing was right. I felt the frustration that I am sure Abraham felt, and at times I felt like giving up (although I understand the magnitude of his situation was much greater than mine, there is a slight parallel). It was from this frustrating path of failed attempts that I learned my own life lesson that timing is everything.

Many of the things predicted for the time of Jubilee are happening on the world stage today. The powers of good versus evil try to destroy our nation from within, making it clear the time is now for the Jubilee Land Plan. We will now focus on the following chapters on the financial side of Jubilee, the forgiveness of debt, and how both sides of Jubilee dovetail into the unmistakable conclusion that timing is everything and the time is now.

# The Origin of the Vision

T he following pages tell a true story of both the largest financial transaction in the history of mankind and the greatest single act of thievery ever committed. This story will reveal a great end-time disbursement of wealth in the form of a modern-day Jubilee, setting the captives free from their enslavement to the financial system of this world and completing one of the final pieces of the prophetic jigsaw puzzle.

The story begins August 4, 1988, as told by our late friend, Brigadier General Wallace "Bud" Kemper, whose patriotic family roots go back to the short-lived Kemper Republic of Northwest Florida in the early 1800s. Ninety days after the Kemper Republic rebelled against Spain, they were annexed by the United States! Many generations later, Wallace would spend twenty years holding positions as president of various banks in Russia under CIA cover. His educational background was accounting, and he spoke the Russian dialect fluently. After his retirement, he settled in Destin, Florida, where he befriended my brother Steve. As we compared stories, we realized he knew all about our story from a different perspective and even provided additional details, among which was the background on the following secret meeting.

Wallace would tell us of what he had heard about a fabled Moscow meeting and a secret meeting in France that kicked off a bizarre chain of events.

\*\*\*\*\*

Rays of sunlight illuminated the cloudy stench of cigar smoke rising to the ceiling of the dimly lit room inside the Kremlin, Moscow.

The mysterious and powerful figures present raised their cognac-filled snifters into the air as a toast to salute the finality of their brilliant plan, which was to be imminently launched onto the world scene. Their plan, known to only those on the inside, was code-named Project Rosebud.

Meanwhile, as the private celebration was taking place in Moscow, at the foot of the French Alps, in the center of a majestic palace nestled on an estate cascading to the south and the east as far as the eye could see, Graham Maurnier, the personal aide to one of the most powerful men in the world, reached the top of the long broad staircase covered in a plush red carpet. The aide softly knocked on the door to the office of Baron Rothchild and proceeded to cautiously enter.

"Baron Rothchild, my lord," said the aide, as he awaited the response of his master, whose high-back brown leather chair was turned facing the window overlooking the countless rows of vineyards on the estate. Silence filled the room as only the sight and smell of the smoke from Baron

Rothchild's pipe could be seen slowly drifting upward in the dark mahogany-walled study. There was no response, so the aide proceeded with great trepidation.

"Baron Rothchild, my lord, please pardon the interruption. We have just received word from Moscow—the signing is complete. The transfer of gold to HSBC is scheduled to begin immediately."

A long pause ensued as the Baron allowed the information to sink in. This was something he had waited a long time to hear, a vision he shared for many years with his elite One-Worlder colleagues.

As he slowly turned his chair around, the expression on his ambitious yet timeworn face was as though a marvelous gift had just been unwrapped and placed on his desk. With a slight twinkle in his eye, he said, "That is good news, Graham, old friend, good news indeed! Keep me posted on the activities. We must ensure the plan is executed flawlessly."

The aide responded, "Yes, my lord."

As he turned to leave the dark study, the baron had one last command. "Oh, and Graham, see to it that we are not disturbed for the time being, will you?"

"Of course, my lord." And with that, the door was quietly closed.

The baron then turned his gaze to his left, where seated in the high-back dark-leather chair, cast in the shadow of the towering bookshelves, was his partner in arms and soon-to-be-leader of the free world, the vice president of the United States of America, George H. W. Bush.

The baron turned to his good friend and said, "Well, Mr. President, I suppose this requires a celebration of our own," and proceeded to pull out his private stock of fifty-year-old King Louis XIV cognac. The baron continued, "I sent a bottle of this special treasure to the meeting in Moscow with a small note attached, which read, 'to be opened only after the ink has dried on the contracts—I trust it will be enjoyed by all.' I would hope our compatriots are raising their glasses as we speak. Let us join with them. Salute! To Project Rosebud!"

This brought a smile to the face of the vice president, as the name and the inception of the project many years ago was credited to none other than himself. As he raised his glass with the baron's in their private celebration, he responded, "Salute! To Project Rosebud indeed!"

The baron said, "Your stature has greatly increased in the eyes of our fellow Brethren. However, there are still some concerns of which you must be aware."

"Concerns?" Bush said. "Such as...?"

The baron pulled open his top desk drawer to remove two of his favorite Cuban cigars and handed one across the desk to his associate, signifying that these concerns were not to interfere with the celebration of the moment. "The consummation of Project Rosebud is contingent upon your election into the White House in November. The mindless masses in America can be extremely fickle."

"Rest assured," Bush confidently responded, "the White House is already mine. We established this with the October Surprise of 1980 when the Iranians agreed to keep the hostages until after the elections in exchange for a few guns." A chilling smile crossed the face of the vice president as he continued, "Furthermore, our spiritual advisors have seen it foretold in the stars, as I'm sure you know."

"Believe me, I am aware of what the advisors have seen. Nevertheless, this is the challenge that faces you presently," the baron said firmly.

"The other challenge is…?" Bush said as he proceeded to light his cigar.

The baron then looked deep into the eye of his apprentice to ensure his point was well made and said, "The other challenge is to keep things quiet while persuading your overzealous and naive Congress to play along. This is the issue most concerning to our fellow Brethren. I have, however, assured them their concerns are securely in your good hands. Please don't prove me wrong."

The vice president smiled and said, "I appreciate your support. The Brethren will soon see it is well founded. The American people and the Congress will see the New World Order, which governs us all, will require a new set of rules as well." Bush then smiled and added, "A new Constitution will be put in place before anyone even notices the old one is gone!"

The baron then smiled and raised his glass in agreement. The two men privately let their minds wander toward the day of fulfillment of their One World Government, their glorious New World Order.

Back in Moscow, the leaders of the Supreme Soviet had just convened an afternoon meeting with an elite group of globalist One-Worlders—Olympians, as they referred to themselves. The name is symbolic of their self-righteous view of their power and ability to control and manipulate events on the world stage from behind the scenes. Their inflated view of themselves was intoxicating to the point they believed themselves as gods. Puppets were, however, in the hands of the god of this world—the prince of the power of the air.

The meeting would forever change the course of history. Over the previous decade, western political and financial leaders, along with hard-liners and reformers of the Communist Empire, held a series of meetings for the purpose of laying the foundation for this historic decision.

The results of these meetings would put in motion a domino effect resulting in the largest financial transaction in history and the greatest theft ever committed by man, forming the core of this story—the true origin of the infamous yet unexplained Federal Budget Surplus, announced to the world by President Clinton in September 2000. The magnitude of the story affected many powerful individuals on a path to the very center of a grand scheme of events, forming the bridge to the global financial power structure of the new millennium.

Headlines unfolded throughout the years regarding the fall of the Iron Curtain and the dismantling of the former Soviet Union. Who could explain the sudden end to the Cold War and the breakup of the only other superpower on the planet? Was this just chance, or was there a design behind the mystery? There were the rise and the totally unexpected collapse of the powerful Southeast Asian economy in the early nineties, the miraculous disappearance of billions of dollars from the US federal budget deficit. Even more miraculous was the appearance of billions of dollars in the budget surplus years of 1999 and 2000, the first in over forty years, sealing President Clinton's legacy as an economic genius. Was there a secret deal that connected these headlines together?

These were mysteries to every "economic expert" around the world. What was the truth behind the rash of mergers of major banks all over the United States, creating monstrous megabanks? Was this just a trend, or was there a deeper, hidden reason? Why did a record number of US Congressmen resign their seats in 1996? Did they have something to hide? Indeed, the secret deal, Project Rosebud, was *the reason* behind these unexplainable headlines.

Over the course of time, the destinies of men and women are determined based on the importance each attaches to an intangible yet razor-sharp veracity forming a constant thread amongst all people, which is known as Truth. The world is a place where, absent of anyone's intended effect on it, Truth exists and is constant, absolute, and unchangeable. All people must, at some point in time, address their relationship with Truth—whether in this life, the next, or both.

Throughout history, people with positions of power, on lease from time, have attempted to change Truth by causing it to conform to their own greed and lustful desires, not taking into consideration the day they would face Truth one-on-one and account for their actions. Attempting to change Truth is like building sandcastles at low tide. The image constructed exists momentarily for all to see, but the constant inevitability of the tide crashing on the shore crumbles the foundation of the facade, and Truth retains its dominance.

So it is with man's attempt to alter and change the appearance of the course of events forming reality. Truth is a power residing in its own dimension outside the control of mortal man. Any attempts to harness and change the very nature of Truth are as feeble as an attempt to change the fundamental nature of water into fire or create darkness from light. Indeed, all things hidden in darkness shall be made manifest in the light. World leaders try to bury the light in the darkness to justify their own greed. But as darkness cannot harness the light, neither can deceit hold the Truth in bondage. For where the River of Truth flows, it brings forth liberty and freedom to the hearts and minds of men.

Revealed in these pages is the single greatest act of theft in the history of mankind, successfully pulled off by the highest level of political and financial leaders in this country, leaders who mortgaged their own eternal future for the short-term gain of money and power in this temporary life. Leaders who had traded their allegiance to the principles of "Freedom and Justice for All" for the privilege of being puppets controlled by the god of this world. Wolves in sheep's clothing they were, failing to grasp a fundamental absolute of the reality in which they live—Truth is a force beyond the control of mortal man.

The financial power brokers behind the scenes have the ultimate financial goal of a one-world currency system. They are the One-Worlders who control and manipulate relationships between nations yet have allegiance to no nation. However, a truly global system could not exist unless the Soviet Union, the other superpower of the twentieth century, was a part of the system as well. The plan was to bring Russia into the game as the first step toward the realization of the goal. The plan's inception began under fellow One-Worlder George H. W. Bush, the director of the CIA in the mid-'70s, and who continued on through his presidency of the United States in the '80s and early '90s. The entire dismantling of the Iron Curtain and the breakup of the former Soviet Union were, by design, part of an elaborate plan. So much hype was made of the free world "winning the Cold War," but the reality was, the Soviet breakup was just one more move in a giant chess game by the puppet masters pulling the strings of events on the world scene. Here now is the inside story.

In the early '70s, after President Nixon, without any objection, removed the gold-backed currency and transitioned to the petrodollar, the price of oil went from three dollars a barrel to thirty dollars a barrel. Arab nations became incredibly rich. Trillions of dollars were deposited in various American banks, as the United States was by far the safest country in the world to invest that kind of money. Inflation was hovering near 20 percent, and the Federal Reserve instructed the major American banks not to loan these funds domestically as it would further add to already out-of-control inflation.

The bankers came up with an extremely dangerous practice of loaning these funds out to various Third World countries, such as Brazil and Argentina. Over the years, it became clear these Third World nations would never be able to repay the loans they were given. New loans were issued to those countries to pay off *only* the interest they owed on the principle of the original loans! These bad loans would be perpetually hidden on their record books, allowing them to annually appear in the black, when in fact, the US banking industry was bankrupt to the tune of $1.7 trillion. It was at this point the One-Worlders needed to pull a rabbit out of a hat, so they devised a plan—Project Rosebud—to bring new life into the flow of the world market currency system. The plan would create trillions of dollars out of thin air, bringing the banking industry back into the black. This later became known to the world as the US Federal Budget Surplus.

In the late '80s, the Soviet Union deposited their national reserves of gold into the Hong Kong and Shanghai Banking Corp. (HSBC) as collateral for the purpose of entrance into the world market currency system. This would be a huge buy/sell deal involving the central banks of Europe and major banks in the US. There was a buying side, a selling side, and a broker in the middle bringing the two sides together. In this case, the broker was the Chicago-based First Central Holding Company (FCHC), whose principal owner was Alex Gaus, a man in his late '60s with twenty-five years in the banking industry. My father, Roger Golden, was his attorney and best friend. The percentage of the fallout was small, but the size and magnitude of the deal created a total dollar amount owed to First Central Holding Company of, ironically, $1.7 trillion!

This was a *legitimate, free-market business transaction*, with a commission involved known as fallout. During the completion of the "Soviet phase" of their scheme, one major irony emerged: Alex Gaus would become the richest man in the world, with wealth exceeding any other individual by hundreds of billions of dollars! Or so it would appear. Because this was not an exchange of policy between nations but rather a legitimate business transaction in the capitalistic world of the free-market currency system, there was no *legal* way for the One-Worlders to stop the due and just payment of $1.7 trillion from landing in the accounts of First Central Holding Company.

Of course, the One-Worlders never had any intention of releasing these funds to their rightful owner, First Central Holding Company. Their intention all along was to seize the funds once they entered the United States, hold on to them, and make money for themselves while they were at it. They would then secretly inject the funds into the banks holding the bad credit notes to the Third World nations, thus stabilizing the US banking industry. The plan called for the payment of funds to travel from Hong Kong through the Central Banks of Europe, arriving in New York at Morgan Guaranty Trust, for disbursement to Standard Charter Bank in Chicago.

One of the most misquoted and misunderstood scriptures of all time is the one about the love of money. "The *love* of money is the root of all evil." Most people state incorrectly that "*money* is the root of all evil," and therefore miss the entire meaning of this important Truth. The way people live their lives in this temporary physical world is merely a proving ground for their trustworthiness and status in the eternal world to come.

All humans are organic beings. Life in the physical world appears as a wisp of vapor that exists for a moment and then quickly vanishes. The choices and decisions made, the state of the heart and the thoughts people think, the way they treat one another, their heart and attitude toward their relationship with God and the principles of his Word—these are all factors that determine their worthiness as they stand before Truth and give an account of their lives.

*Thoughts, actions, words.* Scripture says God created man, above all things, for fellowship. The purpose of sin in Satan's strategy in his war against God is to lead people astray with the deceit of lustful temptations, attempting to accomplish his objectives. By keeping as many people out of fellowship with God as possible, Satan hopes to even the score with God for kicking him out of heaven. He is not mad at God; he is mad at mankind for taking his place as God's favorite.

Once known as Hallel, one of God's most beautiful creations, and one who knows God's ways more than anyone, Satan laughs at people who mortgage their eternal security for *unethical* temporary gain. God states clearly in his Word that wealth and prosperity, along with the right state of the heart, is a good thing. He has no problem with his people obtaining wealth. The problem comes when wealth controls the motives and desires of people. From this point forward, the story known as Plan A is filled with individuals who yield to the temptation of the *love* of money.

Prior to the funds of the fallout arriving in the US, the story finds the first victims of the "love of money" temptation. The last banks in Europe to hold the funds were

Barclay Bank of London and AMRO Bank of Holland. A significant time delay occurred between the release of funds from Barclay and AMRO and the arrival of the funds in Morgan Guaranty Trust Company in New York. An investigation by the World Bank revealed unethical behavior on the part of senior officers of the two European banks. Hands were slapped, heads rolled, and the banks were seriously reprimanded by the World Bank, which represented a type of paradox in the scheme of things.

On the one hand, as a major force in the power structure of the One-Worlders, they were required to see the transaction to its completion to ensure the eventual creation of the One World currency system. On the other hand, they would play an enforcer-type of role, overseeing the safe arrival of the $1.7 trillion into FCHC, requiring the institutions and individuals who thrived on the love of money and greed to keep their hands out of the cookie jar.

Once the web was untangled from Barclay and AMRO, the funds finally arrived in Morgan Guaranty Trust, New York at the end of June 1989. Records will show this was the largest movement of funds into the U.S. that year.

The political and financial inner circles of the greatest country in the history of the world, the United States of America, a country founded on the principles of justice, freedom, and equity, found themselves in quite a dilemma. They basically had two choices: release the funds to FCHC and give up control of their financial system, or illegally withhold the funds. The second choice would require them to act above the law of the land and necessitate illegal and unethical actions, along with massive crimes of coverup and falsehoods. Rumors were quietly making their way through the secret channels of communication that a major movement of funds had arrived in the US. The proper next step in the transaction should have been to immediately move the funds into Standard Charter, Chicago. This was not a government issue. This was a private business transaction completely within the laws of capitalism and free market exchange.

However, the powers that be decided it was necessary for them to hold on to the funds and proceeded cautiously. "Studies" were necessary to determine what effects the release of these funds would have on the economy and the stock market. The communication from the powers that be to Alex Gaus was always, "You're going to get your money, but we've just got to find the best way to handle it before we let you have it."

At one point, the collateral side of the deal broke down, and Alex and Roger had to scramble to save it. The group of men with which Roger had entered the transaction no longer retained their legal position. Roger had maintained his legal position by working with Alex as legal counsel to salvage the deal. His legal background and expertise proved his worth to Alex and was rewarded as the sole legal representative for Alex; he became one of four paymasters with twelve payees under him, all of whom were recipients of varying percentages of commissions from the original $1.7 trillion fallout.

At the same time Roger was securing his position as legal counsel for Alex Gaus in Chicago, the Holy Spirit spoke into my heart while I was in Gulf Breeze, Florida. In a clear and audible voice one evening as I was praying and meditating on scriptures relating to biblical financial principles, the still, small voice inside me suddenly and audibly spoke the word *Jubilee* over and over again: *Jubilee…Jubilee…Jubilee*, nine times in all. The fear of the Lord was upon me, yet there was peace in the depths of my soul. Scripture states the sheep hear their Shepherd's voice. I was positive the Holy Spirit inside me was quietly communicating a message of divine import; however, I would not get the full picture until many years later.

# Timeline of Lies

My father, Roger Golden, was a highly organized, meticulous man. His years in the Navy, as well as his responsibilities as general counsel and secretary in the high-powered corporate world, taught him valuable habits of routine and attention to detail. In his Daytimers, for the last ten years of his life, Roger kept a detailed daily log of the summaries of his communications with the individuals with whom he was involved. An interesting perspective is gained when viewing these notes. A pattern begins to emerge. The records have their own story to tell, a story that follows the timeline of lies issued to Alex.

The pattern goes something like this: at the beginning of the week, the word would be *tomorrow* or the next day at the latest. Friday would roll around and…nothing. The whole sequence would then start over again and some creative excuses were offered to explain the delays. What they were doing was moving the funds out of Continental Illinois over the weekend to make interest on billions and billions of dollars for a few days, before moving them back in at the beginning of the week to make it appear untouched, taking advantage of the Friday-to-Monday loophole in the banking system, all the while undoubtedly laughing at the fact that Alex played along with their clever scheme for so long.

In February of 1989, Alex confirmed to Roger that the origin of the transaction was legitimate, with the news release announcing Russia was going public with their currency. Alex also confirmed he had counseled with an old friend in Chicago, Judge Robert Harris, who assured him the District Court would side with Alex, were the matter to ever land in court.

April, May, and June of 1989 witnessed the power struggle between AMRO Bank and Barclays Bank, as the massive movement of funds arrived in England from HSBC. Barclays tried to divert the funds and was caught by the new bulldog Scotland Yard had recently created in their fraud division. AMRO Bank was then put under the gun to deliver. Howard Neece confirmed to Roger that Barclays made their payout on Thursday, May 11. Vic Strynadka confirmed to Alex that funds had indeed left London, but as a result of Barclays' attempts to divert the funds, they would be going through Chase, not Barclays, NY. Vic Strynadka confirmed the transfer codes to Alex. Barclays, he said, had been wrapped up, and the AMRO transfer would take place next week.

At the end of June, Alex received confirmation of the full transfer of funds going through Chase, London, to arrive in the US through Morgan Guaranty, the largest single transfer of funds into the US in 1989.

As of mid-July, Morgan Guaranty still had the funds and was ordered by the feds to pay immediately. By the end of July, all government agencies had signed off and all funds had moved out of Morgan. August saw the beginning of funds moving in tranches of $250 million at a time from Morgan Guaranty to NY Standard Charter. In early September, Alex received word from the Department of Treasury that everything was approved and by September's end all accounts were to have been credited. On Sunday, October 1, Alex was told that all was on for Monday morning. By Friday, October 6, Alex was still waiting for his call, expecting it at any minute. On October 13, Baron Rothchild told Alex the funds in Standard Charter and First National Chicago had been taxed and everything was in place. Then, Baron added, there was pressure from the world banking community to release the funds immediately. On Monday, October 16, Alex was told Alan Greenspan had given the time of release for two that afternoon.

By the end of November, he was still waiting. Again, the word was that Monday or Tuesday, it should be completed. On December 8, the report was that the FBI cleared the release. On December 15, the feds were moving to credit the First Central account. On December 15, Alex reported that funds were to move into First National Chicago by five and said he expected the final Oval Office confirmation shortly.

Friday, January 5, 1990, the first report of the new decade stated the feds were preparing final release now. The next day, Alex was told the feds deferred to the Oval Office, and the attorney general mandated the feds to approve for distribution Monday or Tuesday. On Saturday, January 11, Alex received word that Monday was the day. Roger decided it was time for him to head to Chicago, feeling the release was imminent. However, ten days later, Roger returned to Florida with the same report he had when he left: "tomorrow is it!"

Friday, January 26, Arthur Anderson (who, a decade later, would be convicted of falsifying records in the giant Enron scandal) was reportedly doing an independent audit, and the final word from within the bank should be done by Sunday. If all went well, they should be ready to go for Monday. Friday, February 2, the word was "all set for next week." The next ten days saw the disappearance of $210 billion. Upon receiving word of this, Alex was furious! He immediately sent a stern warning to the various authorities "in control" of the turnover: The following memo was sent to the CEO of the First National Bank of Chicago regarding the deficit in funds on behalf of the account of First Central Holding Company:

1st February 1990

Gentlemen...

We have been rightfully informed that a definite deficit exists as relates to the above captioned transaction in our behalf. The total amount due at First National Chicago, as relates here, is 1.76 trillion US dollars. The deficit amount cited in communiqué to our office from responsible bank and government sources encompasses an amount of 210 billion US dollars. The deficit amounts are apparently harbored in bank machinations of major banks in the east, which were specified to us in some detail. It is our candid opinion that further transfers from the banks in the east will not be forthcoming, or are subject to indefinite delays, seriously jeopardizing the transaction legally, and in general substance. Said funds (deficit) will not reach our accounts regardless of alleged intrabank commitments or transmission processes.

Accordingly, we proposed to the commissioner of the Internal Revenue Service in Washington, D.C., Comptroller of Currency, Treasury Department, and other government personnel as follows:

1. The face amount due on behalf of First Central Holding Company, Inc., Alex Gaus Jr., is $1,760,000,000,000. (One trillion, seven hundred sixty billion dollars.)
2. Due to the apparent deficit of $210,000,000,000 (two hundred ten billion dollars), the more rightful amount administrable is: $1,550,000,000,000 (One trillion, five hundred fifty billion dollars).
3. Said $210 billion is legitimate income due First Central Holding Company

Inc., Alex Gaus Jr., as captioned
herein.

4. First Central Holding Company Inc.,
Alex Gaus Jr., has proposed (and does
so here legally propose) that $210 bil-
lion amount be assigned to the Internal
Revenue Service Commissioner forthwith as payment and credit against
our final, eventual, tax liability. That
the Commissioner of the Internal
Revenue Service undertake collection
processes against all banks in question
and retain said monies as credit to/for
First Central Holding Company, Inc.,
Alex Gaus Jr., et al.

NOTE: In the event banks in
question forward or transmit funds
to First National Chicago after the
effectual date of this agreement,
said funds would be forwarded to
the Commissioner of the Internal
Revenue Service as payment against
said $210 billion factor.

5. Present equation:
Face amount: $1,760,000,000,000.00
Assignment                    IRS:
$210,000,000,000.00
Net total: $1,550,000,000,000.00
(spendable)

6. To the best of our information, our proposal has been accepted by the Commissioner of the Internal Revenue Service subject only to execution of necessary documentation. That the offices of First National Bank of Chicago have been duly informed or will be so informed during today's working hours.

7. Pursuant to assignment of $210 billion to the Commissioner of the Internal Revenue Service as noted herein, First Central Holding Company, Inc., Alex Gaus Jr., will properly indemnify the bank here, et al, according to law.

8. Thus, 1.5 trillion US dollars will reflect *total net amount* administrable via First Central Holding Company, Inc., Alex Gaus Jr., via/at First National Bank of Chicago.

9. Our best information indicates that, subject to the above set forth, and the execution of necessary documentation, via the bank here and the Commissioner of the Internal Revenue Service, said amount of $1.5 trillion is administrable now.

So, just like that, after waiting a year for his money, Alex Gaus was expected to accept the fact that $210 billion had just vanished! "*Oops!* Sorry! We don't know where we put your $210 billion. We will let you know if it shows up." The arrogance of these people! First, they illegally seize funds from a legitimate, private, free-market business transaction. Then, when they are getting close to releasing the funds (maybe), they expect Alex to just roll over and take it! Alex justifiably said, "No way!" He told the IRS it was coming off the top of their take. "You find out who stole it, and you get it back!" The tax treaty agreements had already been created. The plan was the IRS would get their money first, directly from the accounts of everyone receiving a payout. Once the IRS had received their money, the next step would be the release of the pay orders into the private accounts.

The funds reportedly had magically reappeared, finally making their way back to Chicago. Of course, that required another round of approvals and certifications, which were taking place internally at First National Bank of Chicago, and then the final documents would be prepared.

What had been going on behind the scenes was a complicated maze of smoke and mirrors, intrigue, deception, and mind games at the highest levels of the international playing field. After arriving in Morgan Guaranty in New York, the funds were originally scheduled for Standard Charter Bank of Chicago. After more than a year's worth of unjustifiable delays, the fallout landed at First National Bank of Chicago instead. The funds were then moved to Continental Illinois Bank, not coincidentally right across the street from the Federal Building. Certainly, one of the reasons they chose Continental Illinois was so they could keep an extremely tight grip on things from the Federal Building. The other reason was Continental Illinois just happened to be owned by the FDIC, a result of one of the many casualties of the savings and loan debacle of the eighties.

Continental Illinois was, at that time, the largest bank to go under and the FDIC (actually, the American taxpayer!) bailed them out and took ownership in the process. Howard Neece, one of the individuals on the pay order under Roger Golden, had a close friend at a high level at Continental Illinois named Sue Swank. She became a very valuable source of information Alex and Roger were able to use in their efforts to decipher truth from fiction. All internal activity in Continental Illinois—number crunching, status reports, etc.—was compared against status reports from Washington. Alex also had a close friend at Treasury from whom he was able to get valuable inside information. Both individuals were commonly referred to as "moles" in the communications between Roger, Alex, and Howard Neece to protect the identity and personal well-being of their sources. The moles were as disgusted as Roger and Alex were at the perpetual deception and lack of integrity exhibited by the leaders of America.

Sunday, February 11, Alex was told the bank was funded at 1:30 this a.m. and he expected to be called tomorrow. Tuesday, the word was "tomorrow!" Friday: "We will have confirmation tomorrow." Saturday, February 17, Vic Strynadka reported everything was finalized; First National Bank of Chicago and Federal Reserve were perfecting the details—could hear yet today. Monday, February 19, Alex said Tuesday looked good and he believed he would be called the next day by FNBC. Tuesday's report said Wednesday looked like it! On Friday, February 23, Alex said he was to receive faxes from the Oval Office with instructions over the weekend. The first report of March came on Friday the second. Alex said he expected delivery that night or the next day; the deal was done, and the government officials had gone home. He added he was expecting the courier on Monday. The report from Friday, March 9, was "Next week looks good; the bank is setting aside Monday and Tuesday for us. The feds say next week is ours."

The rest of March and April saw the revelation that Secretary of State Baker and Secretary of Treasury Brady had tried to make a power play and intercept the funds. It was truly one of the most shocking tales exemplifying the greed and corruption evident in the state of events. When the funds originally arrived from Europe, Baker and Brady took it upon themselves to make use of the funds as if the money belonged to them. They opened personal accounts and tried to make their own deal with the Russians. After some time, these actions came to the attention of certain influential individuals at the World Bank and the Central Banks of Europe.

Barber Conable, a former US Marine, congressman, and former chairman of the World Bank, was uncle to Vic Strynadka, one of the original members of the Gaus side of the deal. This proved a valuable connection to Alex as Conable still carried a certain amount of influence. On one hand, there were greedy, high-level US officials trying to steal the transaction. On the other hand, there was Baron

Rothchild, whose family was part of the founding members of the Illuminati generations ago. This was crucial in assisting Alex in his efforts to see the deal to its completion. The interest of Baron Rothchild and the World Bank was for the deal to be done in tranches, and the rest of the tranches could not continue unless the first tranche was completed. Therefore, the Baron became an extremely helpful, albeit unexpected, ally in pressuring Baker and Brady into relinquishing the pursuits of their ill-conceived plans. The International community issued a stern warning, which carried with it the stiff penalty of a verbal slap on the hand.

The rest of the reports through the beginning of May were a series of preparing documents and verifying accounts. Friday, May 4, was to be the final night of receipts exchanged between the Federal Reserve and Continental Illinois. "The Bank was to have finished its major work at 3:00 today, then it will be us shortly." Friday, May 11, Alex said he faxed a plea to President Bush yesterday and he expected to be in the bank today, according to a fax the bank received from Attorney General Dick Thornburgh. Three couriers were reportedly standing by for receipts. Later that day, Alex reported the last three couriers returned at three o'clock from the bank.

Five times during the rest of May, Alex was told "tomorrow." On Friday, June 1, the report was that it was in President Bush's hand for signature. A week later, the president was in Chicago to sign off and "Monday looks good." Wednesday, June 20, Alex was told President Bush signed off at eleven that morning. Thursday, June 28, President

Bush arrived at Continental Illinois at 11:30. The final touches were to be done that afternoon. Tuesday, July 10, the report was that "today should be it." Tuesday, July 24, brought another revelation that the bank had manipulated the accounts. Things, however, looked good for tomorrow.

The next month brought nothing more than week after week of tomorrows until the middle of August, when it was revealed Treasury Secretary Brady was now out of the loop and the new man in charge was White House Chief of Staff John Sununu. The following are documents of communiqués between Alex Gaus and John Sununu, the chief of staff to President George Bush.

*First Central Holding Company, Inc.*
August 3, 1990
FROM: Alex Gaus Jr., Trust Manager
To: John Sununu, esq., Chief of Staff
RE: Communiqué(s) in sequence. Do not intercept—process to Mr. Sununu

Dear Sir…

We have determined that outstanding funds reached our account at Continental Illinois Bank, Wednesday, and Thursday respectively August 2/3, 1990.

That said funds have been properly posted, logged, and registered in the proper trust accounts, and the entire First Central Portfolio is absolutely readied for administration under signature of our office. We were also informed that bank messenger service, as employed by the bank, and at the direction of your office, was dispatched yesterday, Thursday, Aug. 2, 1990—to deliver proper documentation attesting satisfactory transfer—under bonded pouch to our office.

1. Your office is aware that the messenger and his camel never arrived. That said message was further delayed to accommodate other pressure points within government and the condition at Continental Bank.

2. We definitely deduce much of "this" delay is to accommodate the adjournment of Congress, whence questions will be minimized.

3. We have no difficulty working with Continental Bank. However, our original account, where to our income was to be transmitted from the banks in Europe, via Morgan Trust, was Standard Charter Bank, Chicago. In the fraudulent processes of the Comptroller of Currency and employees of the Federal Reserve Banking Systems, that bank was "slaughtered" and thereafter, the Comptroller

danced from bank to bank to cover irregularities of his office.

4.  Your office, and the integrity of your office, is cognizant that funds we are claiming consist of income "earned." We did not work for the government, whence the government or its employees can determine withholding payment for fulfillment of contracts or agreements. The government, or any service entity is not "pay-master" hereunder, and has absolutely no right, within the parameters of all government regulations, and the laws of this country to withhold our income.

5.  The employees of the government, in varied capacities, used positions of employment of delegated authority to "short stop," and divert funds that did not belong to such parties or persons, to cause income therefrom, for varied reasons and placement thereof, in varied projects, special interest groups, personal accounts…none of which reached the general fund of the Treasury from where the American Citizenry would have benefit.

6.  Employees of government's agencies circulated documents into banks of the United States and other parties argu-

ing that our income was non-existent, and was a fraudulent representation on the part of First Central Holding Company, Inc., Alex Gaus, Jr., the Central Banks of Europe, etc. We demanded that parties at the offices of the Comptroller of Currency and the Federal Reserve Systems reduce their statements to writing, wherethrough there was a record actionable in the courts…they refused.

7. Legally, the employees of the government, that so engaged, have no right to either absolute, or qualified immunity under the law. They argue the right or are acting on behalf of orders from "upstairs." Either the complete documentation from our Mandate employers in Europe are fraudulent, or the employees at varied government levels have deliberately lied or are absolutely guilty of criminal statute: 18 USC S2314—and conspiracy as relates thereto.

8. If I walk into the bank this afternoon and demand to administer our earnings, what will their reception be?

God Bless!

Alex Gaus, Jr.

cc: Comptroller of Currency—Clarke

*First Central Holding Company, Inc.*
August 6, 1990
FROM: Alex Gaus, Jr., Trust Manager
TO: John Sununu, et al., Chief of Staff
RE: Communiqués in sequence. Last prior—08/03/90

Dear Sir: Please accept this communicate as our official demand for payment of our funds as noted in previous communications. As relates to the above captioned reference:

1. Funds were earned by First Central Holding Company Inc., and Alex Gaus, Jr., trust manager, pursuant to mandate, effected via Central Banks of Europe, legal and political parties thereto.

2. Persons and parties in the United States Government as employees, appointees, or its elected officials, had no right or claim against said earnings.

3. Persons and parties within the confines of the United States Government, in varied capacities, acted in fraud against First Central Holding Company, Inc., and Alex Gaus, Jr., to divert said earnings for other purposes and accounts, including their own personal use, con-

trary to the laws of the United States of America. Furthermore, said parties, and persons, committed fraud, and the criminal acts evident herein under color of the appointed, elected offices, and those encompass in civil service to the United States, being compensated for said employment, via the tax dollars contributed by the American Citizenry.

4. Said persons and parties, elected or otherwise appointed/employed, did not represent the acts of the United States Government, or the decrees of Congress, while engaged in commitment of fraud. Said persons and parties cannot claim immunity under color of their capacities; have thereby entered the government into said acts; have acted in collusion with each other, implicating agencies, departments, and persons, without the knowledge of the true Government of the United States. Congress was not informed, or petitioned, to withhold earnings of the American Citizenry, by persons so employed, pursuant to fraudulent and questionable methods.

5. Said governments parties and persons, deliberately included, and/or solic-

ited, the cooperation of United States banks in varied forums, along with other world banks in furtherance of illegal activity…invoking the wrath of both civil and criminal Rico sanctions. [See Thornburgh's announcement of recent indictments in Chicago against traders and Commodity and Mercantile Exchanges.]

6. Illegal acts manifest here are/were not pursuant to executive, legislative, or judicial requisites, where under said government's persons and parties were illegally authorized, as a matter of law, or as a matter of preferential political position, to illegally manipulate (for their own good), earnings not belonging to said governments parties and persons, in an attempt to confiscate same through methods of concealed theft.

7. Where banks co-conspired and participated in overt acts, with governments, persons, and parties in unlawful administration of said earned funds, including, however, but not limited to:

   a) Construction of fictitious accounts.

b) Divergent monies and interest earned there against to private and cloaked accounts.

c) Transferring, illegally, and under color of government's office, funds, to varied accounts, across state lines, under clandestine account numbers and codes.

d) Under the guise of government undertakings, pursuant to acts of Congress, while earned funds were being manipulated and spent in obvious fraud...

The same legal sanctions are invoked, as under the unlawful laundering of funds, as apply to drug crimes and other types of criminal conspiracy. [Review your textbooks as to the spectrum of conspiracy sanctions; see *Corpus Juris Secundum* for your own enlightenment.]

8. The record will show that on February 1, 1990, this office forwarded telecommunique to Federated Chicago Corp., First National Bank of Chicago, et al., with copies to: Commissioner of the Internal Revenue Service, the Comptroller of the Currency, the

Secretary of the Treasury, with like copies to the Central Banks of Europe Mandates, being fully aware, and factually informed, in all detail, as to the "goings-on" of said persons and parties in government, who acted illegally, and under color of their government trust, while so engaged:

a) We proposed with full legal design, our assignment of outstanding concealed funds as applied to our earnings…to the Internal Revenue Department, for collection, with agreement to apply the proceeds of said collection to any future tax liability that may be incurred. Re: FCHC, Gaus; and that said funds be shown in the general fund of the United States Treasury for the benefit of the American Citizenry.

b) IRS remained moot to our proposal. Their office was not ignorant of the "Glockenspiel" in concert.

9. We are further aware that our goodwill has been interpreted as a weakness; our Christian approach as an object of ridicule, and political humor, by said

persons and parties within the broad spectrum of the entity we referred to as Government.

Best stop laughing!

a) There is no person in the Cabinet structure immune from legal sanctions as relates to here, where there is fraud or questionable activity involved against the people.

b) There is no person in the Cabinet structure, or any other governmental capacity, who may invoke an umbrella of the Office where under, to act illegally, to obtain fraudulent gain; to violate the Constitutional Mandates afforded the American people or the Civil Rights thereunder.

c) Parties and persons, within the confines of said government entities or functions, cannot contemplate relief, pursuant to any statute of limitations law, civil or criminal.

10. We know from whence our earnings were obtained, and how we honorably earned same. We know of "their bouncing around" after arrival in the

United States. Contrary to all reports and promises, we know where the funds are today. We find that most "game players," herein, are exposed.

Respectfully submitted, we believe your decision is obvious!

Gaus

*First Central Holding Company, Inc.*
August 8, 1990
From: Alex Gaus, Jr., Trust Manager
To: John Sununu, et al., Chief of Staff
Re: Communiqué(s) in sequence.

Dear Sir:

We have been properly advised all the funds have been accounted for and are in the custody of the Trust Department, Continental Bank, et al., processed for legal notification to/for our office:

1. All dollar credits are accounted for, totaling 1.76 trillion US dollars... [some small amounts may still be in "some transit form"—however, are specifically accounted for by the Comptroller of the Currency, and the Federal Reserve Banking Systems, and are considered as administrable by the account...and are not legal, or regulatory basis, for delay or procrastination.]
2. Continental Bank is no longer the "escrow" bank for the foregoing entities, where through our funds have been "shuffled." Further hereto, Continental Bank, et al., will not disclaim the account, or publish misleading statements to First Central

Holding Company, Inc., Alex Gaus, Jr., and will (according to state's trust laws), properly notify First Central Holding Company, Inc., Alex Gaus, Jr., forthwith.

3. Final trust receipt, or applicable banking documentation, customary as between the Comptroller of the Currency, to the Trust Department of Continental Bank, et al., will be executed forthwith, this date, and the funds rightfully belonging to First Central Holding Company, Inc., Alex Gaus, Jr., will be fully surrendered, as required by law. Our position, as it relates to Continental Bank, is noted in our previous communiqué to your office, and the office of Janet Walton, dated August 3, 1990. Our legal position has not changed, as relates to the misadministration of our earnings, noted in detail, in our previous communiqués.

Alex Gaus, Jr.

cc: Comptroller of Currency—Clarke

*First Central Holding Company, Inc.*
August 8, 1990
Continental Bank Corp. & Continental Bank, N.A. Chicago, IL 60697

Attention: Thomas Theobald, Chairman
[Also, Trust Department, et al.]
FROM: Alex Gaus, Jr., Trust Manager
RE: EFG JACOBE/ICC400/322/C3416
Enclosed communiqués: John Sununu,
White House,
Comptroller of the Currency—Clarke
Funds (earnings) 1.76 trillion U.S.D.

Gentlemen...

Please accept the enclosures for the record.

We are satisfied our current information, received from within the government's sources and offices, is accurate, and the account captioned above, has been readied in the Trust Department at Continental Bank.

Without further explanation, our correspondence with Mr. Sununu, et al., and the offices of the Comptroller of Currency is clear to understand. Based on all the information we have garnered, it may be that Continental has been contacted by other government's representatives, independent of our office. However, the dilemma lies squarely with government's employees, and/or persons in political, and appointed positions. We have not attempted to determine whether

Continental was afflicted by the manipulation we experienced.

We believe Continental, its Trust Department, is in a position to commence mutual administration of our earnings now. Pursuant to reports from the government's persons, we anticipate your notification of completed accounts, etc., soonest. If you have any questions regarding our communiqué here, you may contact our office, or you may contact "Big John" at the White House.

Respectfully,
Alex Gaus, Jr.

Sununu reportedly signed off on the turnover at six on Friday, August 17. On Thursday, August 30, Alex reported he was expecting to get word later that evening. The report from Tuesday, September 4, was that Alex "should be able to sign documents tomorrow." The month of September ended with Alex cheerfully reporting the bank had completed its work that day. On October 18, Alex reported the bank workers finished at 2:30. Thursday, November 1, Alex said everyone was working hard; "tomorrow should see good things."

Friday, November 9, Alex said all was looking good for Tuesday. Wednesday, November 21, was to be the announcement of the turnover, with the administrative work being done on Monday and Tuesday. Tuesday, November 27, Alex reported the bank takeover was to happen on Thursday. Tuesday, December 11, Alex said everything was progressing nicely; work should be done that week. Saturday, December 15, Alex told Roger the week was full of political sniping, but everything was completed at four the day before, including the FDIC turnover. The time was reportedly set but not disclosed. Wednesday, December 26, Alex was expecting the FDIC turnover people, due to arrive shortly from D.C. Thursday, December 27, the last report of the year was merely that the final countdown had begun!

How wrong they were. As the years passed and the funds were still held captive, the whereabouts of the captivity became more and more clear. In the mid-'80s, there was another major victim of the S&L Crisis. The FDIC had already bailed out Continental Illinois and could not afford to bail out another large bank, so they made a deal with North Carolina National Bank (NCNB), a relatively unknown bank on the national scene. The Republic Bank of Texas was on the verge of going under, and the deal between the FDIC and NCNB was that NCNB would buy out the Republic Bank of Texas in exchange for a favor in the future. The favor in the future turned out to be the privilege of holding on to the fallout money for an extended period of time, resulting in its rise to national prominence over a relatively short period of time.

NCNB invested the funds in the Japanese economy and other various markets making exorbitant amounts of interest and then—*bam!* Out of nowhere, NCNB merged with C&S/Sovran Bank in Atlanta to form NationsBank, America's fifth largest bank. Throw in a couple of beautiful, majestic skyscrapers in Atlanta and Charlotte, and there was a nowhere-to-everywhere story that is every bank chairman's fantasy. NationsBank would soon be bought out by BankAmerica, the primary tool used by the globalists in their execution of their plan, as they illegally purchased Continental Illinois for $2 billion, when the false assets of Continental Illinois were listed at $22 billion.

Another dimension of the corrupt nature of the story is the Truth behind the method the Bush Administration used in illegally arming Iraq. In the late seventies, the former shah of Iran had all but put a halt to the all-important flow of opium from the Illuminati-controlled poppy fields of India and Pakistan through Iran and into the gateway of the west to the processing plants on the shores of Monaco. As a result, the One-Worlders then installed the radical regime in Iran, who agreed to let the flow of opium continue to the west if the flow of weapons continued into Iran, which already possessed a military armed with state-of-the-art weaponry from the previous regime. Once the Iran–Iraq war began, the One-Worlders realized they needed to strengthen Iraq and its outdated Soviet military hardware, so a full-scale effort began to illegally arm Iraq to "stabilize" the region.

These actions were illegal because under the Carter Administration, Iraq had been declared by Congress to be a nation that supported terrorism and therefore unable to legally receive weapons sales from the US. Iraq became the Bush Administration's new best friend. Billions and billions of dollars poured into Iraq through illegal government-backed grain sales and loans, which subsequently sold the wheat to Russia. Iraq, of course, never paid back a cent of these funds, which were again left to the American taxpayer to absorb.

As far as two weeks before the Gulf War of 1990, the Bush Administration was still trying to get another $500 million of illegal loans to Iraq pushed through Congress. In the desert sands of ancient Persia, millions of lives and billions of dollars were wasted on the One-Worlders' manipulation of nations. The seeds of betrayal the Bush Administration sewed against Iraq would later come back to haunt them. President Bush, himself a loyal subject of the One-Worlders, felt free to sling an ocean of cash he considered to be his own in any direction he wished.

Washington was out of control. They had stolen the keys to the candy shop, and all the bigwigs were getting fat. Everyone was making money off Alex's money except Alex, who by this point had had enough. He took his case to Barber Conable, the former chairman of the World Bank after serving as a US Marine and NY Congressman. Conable was able to persuade the World Bank to act on behalf of First Central Holding Company. In 1991, a writ of mandamus complaint was filed with Judge Gerhard Gesell of the Federal District Court in Washington D.C., who issued a ruling in favor of Alex Gaus and First Central Holding Company. The court order demanded full release of the original $1.76 trillion, *plus interest, penalties, and interest on penalties*, on said amount from the past three years. The government appealed Judge Gesell's ruling all the way to the Supreme Court, who had no legal choice but to uphold his ruling in light of all the evidence.

On October 7, 1992, the US Supreme Court issued their decree to the Federal Reserve, the lower courts, and the World Bank to release the funds to FCHC. The total amount now owed to First Central Holding Company was well *in excess of $7 trillion*! According to the mandate from the Supreme Court, 1,600 banks were now in a debt position to Alex Gaus and First Central Holding Company! There was not a major player in the United States banking community who was not a member of the group now indebted to one man!

Washington insiders were now scrambling for cover. No one expected the entire thing to end up in the courts. The One-Worlders were furious with Judge Gesell for allowing the writ into his courtroom in the first place. Now there was a Supreme Court Order declaring ownership of the United States Banking industry to First Central Holding Company.

The One-Worlders arranged an elaborate repayment plan that included an assortment of stocks, bonds, treasury notes, and cash, but it was all centered around Alex taking ownership of Continental Illinois Bank. The FDIC was eager to unload Continental Illinois anyway, thus cleaning out the last remnants of the nightmarish S&L crisis. Alex was asked to be patient, as if he had not already been, in awaiting his money while the feds put the whole package together. There would be numerous "dry runs" to ensure all monies were accounted for and to ensure that, in handing over control of the banking industry, all of the banks were on the same page and there was no foul play.

What they were really doing all this time was white-washing all the computer records to ensure there were no paper trails. Massive whitewashing! Alex was "required" to sign numerous concessions. The IRS would get an exorbitant amount more money than originally agreed to, now that Alex was getting so much more, of course. Alex was asked to agree not to prosecute any of the guilty parties once the funds were turned over. Months' and months' more delays ensued, all in the name of "getting the turn-over ready."

Prior to the Supreme Court ruling in favor of FCHC in October of 1992, but after Judge Gesell's court order mandating the release of the funds to First Central Holding Company, the timeline of lies continued. On Wednesday, March 4, Alex reported it was all mechanically done. He said the FDIC and Continental Bank details were completed the day before and the feds gave their final release with credits being transferred in until seven. First Central should be set the next day. Thursday, March 5, the report was that everything was focusing on ten tomorrow. Throughout the end of March, eight more times the word coming from Alex to Roger was, essentially, "tomorrow looks good."

April 1, the report was that everyone was working that night to finish. April 6, Alex was expecting word "any minute." Tuesday, April 7, Alex was expecting stock transfers to be completed by midnight. April 9, the word was that preparation for closing was taking place and Treasury people were in the bank. Tuesday, April 14, Alex said everything should finish that night. The next day, he reported "we should be next. The Treasury people finished at two."

Monday, April 20: "still waiting." Monday, April 27, Alex said he understood it was done but no word yet. Tuesday, he told Roger the lawyers were back in judges' chambers. On Wednesday, the report was that the final modified court order was completed and it was "generally in our favor."

The activity of the month of May was filled with reports like "the attorney general is wrapping up the mandate of court order." The court approved closing statement from the attorney general's office, and the last report from May was that the court said all requirements have been met.

Monday, June 22, Alex reported that everything was finished. Two days later, the federal marshals arrived in Chicago at five with all final hard copies of the court order mandating the release of funds. A month later, the court was pushing for "tomorrow." Tuesday, July 21, the court said everything finalized at four; Alex said, "We are next." On Friday, they were still waiting.

August saw a flurry of activity from the courts, beginning on Monday, August 3, when he was expecting the word shortly. August 10, Alex said, "All is done." Two days later the judge said, "Be patient, your call is coming." On Friday, August 14, Alex reported that the World Bank lawyers had a copy of final court order, yet on Monday the judge called and said the World Bank counsel in D.C. told them just a minor adjustment needed to be made and they would call Chicago to give them time for Gaus to be in bank for closing. Thursday, August 20, Alex said, "Tonight should be it." Friday, he expected the word by seven. Monday's report was that everything was done. Tuesday, August 25,

Alex said he was with the judge most of the day; today was the first day in a week the judge was not in the bank. Wednesday, Alex was expecting a copy of the court order shortly. He was told the judge was finished. The last day of August, Alex said he worked all day and things could be ready at any moment.

Friday, September 4, saw another court modification. On September 8, Alex said he had worked all weekend and should hear from court that night. The next day, he said everything was now completed and he was awaiting a call from the judge. Tuesday, the fifteenth, Alex said it was in the hands of Seventh Circuit Court and on Friday he was expecting stock transfers. The reports from Monday and Wednesday of the following week were that the court was still working on it but it looked very promising.

On Thursday, September 24, it was reported the remaining bank officers had asked the court for indemnity from prosecution for their actions, and the court agreed. By Monday, the court was still working on bank officers' hold harmless agreement. Tuesday, September 29, Alex was told the bank officers were on their way out and that the World Bank had admonished the Seventh Circuit Court, demanding a clean sweep for "take one."

Saturday, October 3, Alex reported the court finished its review the day before. Monday's word was that "all is ready." On Wednesday, October 7, Alex said a significant thing happened that day: "the Supreme Court ruled in our favor!" The order was sent to the White House, the Federal Reserve, and the lower courts. On Thursday, Alex was working with lower courts regarding transfer. Tuesday,

October 20, Alex reported the Supreme Court order went to Seventh Circuit Court and was being implemented. On Wednesday, Alex confirmed that the Seventh Circuit had it and he was expecting word yet that night. On Monday, October 26, Alex was still waiting on courts. Wednesday, he said he should know in twenty-four hours. Thursday, Alex reported that the Supreme Court justices were in Chicago, and on Friday the thirtieth he said he met with them all day and the court now had it to where any other adjustments required his approval.

November 3 of 1992 saw the election of Bill Clinton to the Oval Office. Even though the full Supreme Court was in Chicago, working through Friday the thirteenth, and reports continued to come in that everything should close shortly; the reality was that the new administration now had the keys to the cookie jar and they were going to take their time to make sure they thoroughly uncovered all the details of what had been taking place the last four years. If there was something in it for them, they were intent on getting it. There was the occasional "court finished today; looks good for tomorrow" report that came in, but for the most part, the transition from one administration to the next kept things slow through inauguration day of 1993.

Then on Wednesday, January 27, Alex reported things might have finished today; for the last couple of days seventeen persons from the office of the Controller of Currency have been in Continental Illinois. The report may have sounded positive but was the first step in the Clinton hunting hounds sniffing out fresh blood. Through the first several months of the year, Alex continued to receive reports such as "finished with courts; tomorrow should see the start of the bank work," "court is finished," "court mandates dribbling down," "court is done; bank is carrying out mandate," "last adjustments by Federal Reserve," "court proceeding with enforcement," and "court mandate will be incorporated in trust agreement." Then on Tuesday, May 11, Alex reported that the Supreme Court approved the administrative judges' work. He also reported something interesting—President Clinton wanted to see the judge but was turned down.

Thursday, May 13, Alex reported, "We are close! The decree has been drafted and approved and the press release is being constructed." Wednesday, Alex said the final Federal Reserve account was put into First Central. "We should be in tomorrow."

On Friday, May 21, the court reportedly received the final commitments from the Federal Reserve. On Thursday, May 25, the feds were wrapping up details. On June 1, Alex said he was waiting on a call from court: "everything is set and ready." Thursday, June 3, Alex reported Friday and Saturday should see funds dispersed! Friday's report was that Alex was expecting a copy of the court order soon, adding it should be happening on transfers. Tuesday, June 8, Alex was told the transfers should start at 11:00 a.m. tomorrow! Wednesday, June 9, the court had to make one last record adjustment. Tuesday, June 15, Alex was told "tomorrow should be it."

Friday, June 18, Alex was told the court was preparing his invite and all the work was done. Monday, June 28, Attorney General Janet Reno said, "All is set." The month of

June ended with a familiar report: "tomorrow!" Thursday, July 8, Alex was told that Reno's time extension was up that day and she notified the courts and the feds that the record was now complete. Friday, Alex was told the turnover was in process. Wednesday, July 14, Alex said the district court was proceeding; the record was being perfected. Thursday, he said the record was almost done. Monday, July 19, the bank was to receive the final administration from courts. July ended with Alex still waiting on the court order.

Monday, August 2, Alex was told the courts were still working on window time. Sources included the World Bank legal counsel in D.C. and the District Court, Chicago. Tuesday, August 3, Alex was told the IRS had to take one more look at how to take taxes; the issue could be resolved that night. Monday, August 9, Alex was told the feds were releasing funds at midnight. Then on Tuesday, August 24, he was told the final approval of settlement agreement was to be completed shortly. On Thursday, all signatures were to be on the final settlement agreement by 8:00 p.m. that night. On Monday, August 30, Alex said the notice was on the way. Tuesday the thirty-first, Alex was told the judge had it in full control for release.

Friday, September 3, Alex was told the Supreme Court was with closing group drafting details—should be completed yet that night. Wednesday, September 8, the word was that all should be ready by 6:00 p.m. that night. A week later, the report was the same—the window is ready.

On Thursday, September 16, Roger received a call from Howard Neece, who reported Sue Swank, his mole contact at Continental Illinois, told him that a banker who is now out of the deal said, "This is the scam of the year! The bank will give window time, then not honor it! The banks have enough money they feel they can do anything and get away with it!" Deep down in their hearts, Roger and Alex knew this to be true, yet they pressed on, hoping against hope their faith, hard work, and perseverance would pay off. Yet the timeline of lies continued. The month of September ended with a deadline for turnover mandated by Attorney General Reno.

October of 1993 saw the creation of yet another Supreme Court memo, which was to arrive in Chicago any minute. The FDIC was to send a commission to represent their end of the turnover. By the end of the month, the new and improved court orders were issued, but of course Janet Reno had to approve the final draft. Alex expected to have his copy of the memo any minute, at which time all would once again be done.

On Wednesday, November 3, the Supreme Court took charge with a three-justice panel. They immediately removed the federal people and told Alex he was to be called in "tomorrow." On Friday, there was a freeze put on all accounts, and Alex was told Monday was the day. On Wednesday, November 10, Alex signed off on more consent agreements to complete the deal. He was told Attorney General Reno should have the documents ready by seven. On Monday, November 15, the freeze on the accounts was lifted, and the Supreme Court closing panel arrived in Chicago on Thursday.

On Tuesday, December 28, Alex was still waiting, but he was told the Supreme Court issued writ of execution the day before and he should be in the bank tomorrow.

On Monday, January 3, 1994, Howard Neece called Roger to inform him the mole at Continental Illinois said that distribution was set for that week. Alex spent the rest of the month in the hospital. With his heart functioning at ten percent of its capacity, a bout with pneumonia in Chicago in the middle of January was the last thing he needed. A personal nurse was assigned to take care of Alex at his home to help him regain his strength, which he did. At the end of January, he received a report that BankAmerica had been brought into the picture as part of Reno's plan and everything was back on track that week.

Tuesday, February 15, Howard Neece reported the mole said an exceptionally large block of stock was transferred to Alex Gaus yesterday. The deal appeared to be done. On Wednesday, Roger found out Alex had been in hospital since Friday but was recently released and doing much better now. On Friday, Alex reported the government should be done within the hour and he was expecting documents via courier that evening. For the next three months, Alex was in and out of intensive care in the hospital. The doctors had forbidden him to be involved in anything remotely related to work. There was grave concern on the part of all that Alex had simply been worn down by the constant deceit practiced by the federal authorities. Perhaps that was actually their plan.

The individual who played the role of the mole at Continental Illinois Bank was an old friend of Howard

Neece. Their friendship was formed through a business relationship, and over the years they had kept in touch; valuable information was provided as a result. All the high-level machinations of the bank, with regards to movements of funds and the various high-ranking officials frequently in and out of the bank, were communicated to Alex and Roger through Howard Neece. This was extremely important because one of the major areas of concern, for the powers that be, was the whole issue of what to do with Continental Illinois. Alex Gaus had legally been given ownership of Continental Illinois Bank as part of the plan for the turnover of his funds, which were illegally seized by the leaders of America, land of the free.

As the whitewashing of records continued, the "powers that be" had to come up with a plan to make the issue of Continental Illinois disappear as well. This is where BankAmerica entered the picture as a major player. During the three months in 1994 Alex spent hospitalized, there was a public announcement made stating that the stock of Continental Illinois was purchased by BankAmerica. Alex was told this was a mere formality to eliminate the possibility of questions being raised in the business community regarding how one man could possibly come from nowhere to purchase a bank the size of Continental Illinois. Alex was told his money was still coming, but the sale of stock to BankAmerica was necessary to deceive the public.

Alex was forced to go along with their game, to get his money. The choice he made was to cooperate; all he wanted was what was rightfully his. It was not his desire to legally take on the government. So BankAmerica was richly rewarded for their role in the giant scandal, as they would be purchased by NationsBank, then purchased Security Pacific, to later become Bank of America, vaulting them into the top four of the banking community. This was yet another link in a long line of deceptions.

It was now the middle of May, and there were reports surfacing that the Senate Banking Committee was raising questions into the affairs taking place in Chicago. On Monday, June 13, 1994, Alex was back home and had received word that he was scheduled to be in the bank tomorrow. Ten days later, he was told the feds were ready to turn things over by—you guessed it—tomorrow. Friday, July 22, Alex was told he would receive, tonight or tomorrow, the final approval of calculations and coordinates of distribution. Reports came in the rest of the year stating the window times were set; the final adjustments to the tax treaty had been made, and the Supreme Court had set the time for turnover. Thirteen more times, he was promised tomorrow. "You'll be spending money on Friday."

On December 28, President Clinton sent word that he wanted the deal done before the Republicans took over Congress in January. Saturday, January 7, 1995, the word came to Alex that everything was ready, and it was just political now, as if it had not been political all along. Alex found himself in the hospital again at the beginning of April with fluids and heart congestion. He was battling the political/financial power structure of America and struggling against the onslaught of death at the same time. He would survive another round, however, as on Tuesday April 13, 1995, Alex received word that three Supreme Court justices (Scalia, O'Connor, Ginsburg) had signed off on the release of funds to First Central Holding Company. This is where the value of relationships is revealed.

It was stated earlier that when people's lives are over, they will be remembered by the relationships they had with the individuals they interacted with throughout the course of their lives, the thousands of people in which they come in contact over the course of time. Some stay, some fade away. Put them all together on a screen, with each one forming a pixel, and a picture will emerge.

Through the words people speak and their methods of interaction, the Lord networks these relationships. He opens some doors and closes others as people travel down the path that is their life. Alex Gaus met many people throughout the course of his life, from the days of his disciplined, religious upbringing (his father being a Moravian preacher), through the days he spent as an OSS agent in World War II, the twenty-five years he spent in the banking industry, and into his years of presently owning and operating his own brokerage house. Certainly, Alex's life was filled with individuals whose paths crossed his, some of greater significance than others. Sometimes relationships exist then fade away or become dormant for a while before surfacing again.

Imagine flying in a plane, looking down to see two roads whose paths cross go their own direction for a while and then meet again. Such was the case with "the mole." Alex and the mole had known each other for years with the time Alex had spent in the banking industry. Years would pass without much interaction between the two, and then their paths would cross again, carrying much greater significance the second time around. The mole, known to Alex as Jane, had gone to work for the United States Treasury Department and was privy to significant, valuable, high-level information behind the scenes.

People around the world were startled as to the incredible growth that took place in the Japanese economy in the mid-'90s. The majority of the top ten largest banks in the world were, at one time, Japanese. Indeed, the Southeast Asian economy, in general, was the hot spot for investors for many years.

One of the things Alex learned from the mole was that the people in control of *his* money had chosen the Southeast Asian market as "their target of choice" with which to make money from their illegal seizure of the trillions of dollars. For years, the pattern banking was to show internal bank records to reflect the funds as presently accounted for at the beginning of the week in the accounts of First Central Holding Company. They would then turn around and loan the funds out for investment in the various markets, the majority being Southeast Asian. Alex would receive word he was to be called in to the bank for turnover "tomorrow," or Monday, or whenever. Bank records would then be adjusted to show all funds presently accounted for, all the while never intending to release the funds.

One of the sad stories resulting from this pattern of "show me the money" was the truth behind the death of Clinton White House deputy counsel Vincent Foster. Foster and good friend Webster Hubbell came to Washington with the Clintons, both having served Gov. Clinton in some capacity in Arkansas. Both were rewarded with their own piece of the pie with individual accounts. Foster reportedly went to check on his account during a time in the shell-game pattern of moving the money around and realized his account was empty. Enraged, he went to his good friend Webster Hubbell demanding answers.

Hubbell tried to calm him down and explain what was going on, but Foster would have none of it and threatened to blow the whistle. The result was a reported suicide as Foster's body was found by the US Park Police in the woods inside one of the city parks where the Park Police maintained authority, not the city police.

The Park Police earned the reputation as the Keystone Cops as they stood fast on their declaration of suicide, even though there was a bullet wound to the head but no blood on Foster's white shirt, no dirt found on his shoes from walking into the woods, and his car was found in the parking lot, but no keys were found in the car or on Foster's body.

These were just some of the suspicious facts of the case, and one example of how deadly the game was being played by Washington's high-level powerbrokers. The temptation of the love of money, greed, power, and control all had an iron grip around the leaders of the nation. The mole at the Department of Treasury began to receive disturbing reports revealing the truth of events taking place behind the scenes. Several letters arrived at Alex's office while he lay half-dead in a hospital bed, just after the Supreme Court justices had signed off on the release.

February 24, 1995

Dear Mr. Gaus:

Since Secretary Brady is in Reno, and we have a hard time contacting him, and I do not want to discuss this on the hotel line, I am taking the liberty of sending this to you.

I have been advised, by our usually reliable contacts, the banks involved were told on Wednesday to ignore the trusts and instructions and all court orders regarding them.

I understand while Chairman Greenspan was on Capitol Hill this week to talk about interest rates, he tried, on Wednesday, to strike a last-minute deal that he would not raise interest rates, but would release the tax funds if Congress and President Clinton would jointly demand the Supreme Court allow him to retain control of the World Bank funds and your funds. I hear he was told the Congress and the President have no authority to demand anything of the Supreme Court. I hear he then tried to make a deal with the Court that the funds for foreign governments would be released. The actual cash available to be released to you, but he and Secretary Rubin would remain in control of all the state trusts and the bank. Greenspan absolutely refuses to release control of those 1,600 banks to you. And the thought of you selling thirty-year mortgages at 6 percent is devastating. He and Secretary Rubin are determined to find a way to deny control of those banks to you. I understand these items are the basis for the Court wanting to meet with the World Bank attorneys. I also hear while the Supreme Court was trying to broker a deal, they stand firmly committed to release of the funds to rightful owners.

My contact feels if the deal is not completed by Monday night, after all of the maneuvering of the last two weeks, it will take the actual physical arrest and arraignment of Greenspan before the Federal and State Banks will proceed with the court orders. The banks do not want to release the funds until their boss, Greenspan, the Chairman of the Fed, approves the release or is removed from office. I also hear Senator Simon is terribly upset by this happening in Illinois banks, and about all the tax funds taken by the State and not applied to purposes benefiting the citizens of Illinois. He is afraid he will be caught up in the storm and he expects his reputation will be destroyed when the information becomes public.

Note: I removed the names of the sending party(s). I have the identity, etc., if publication becomes necessary. However, I will only reveal the "originator" of the information with the "supplier's" permission.

Sincerely,

Jane

March 10, 1995

Dear Mr. Gaus:

I have been unable to learn much about the "list of perpetrators." However, I do have some information for you.

The list is being held closely by the Supreme Court, as they do not want it in the public domain and the Court staff has been warned to hold the information closely. There may be thirty-seven names on the list, and it reaches into "high places." Discussions on how to handle the indictments and/or arrests and the timing are being held between the Court and the Justice Department.

Sincerely,<br>Jane

March 10, 1995

Dear Mr. Gaus:

I hear there has been no change of attitude since my fax of Feb. 25, 1995.

Particularly, Rubin has tied his future to that of Greenspan: they will sink or swim together. It is still all or nothing for them.

Reference the Thursday meeting with the Supreme Court: I hear Rubin was told he will be arrested by warrant, charging him with one or more felonies, and he will go to federal prison if he does not immediately cease and desist from his activities flouting Supreme Court orders. I have been unable to identify the names on the list of offenders.

I hear at Treasury that Rubin and his top officers are fully knowledgeable about all of the actions regarding this case and will stand or fall together. They all know they are defying Supreme Court orders and committing collusion and conspiracy, but they do not care. They believe indictments are probable, but "the Treasury Department never does anything wrong, and we always do what is best for the US Banking community." The details seem to be open knowledge on the "working level" at Treasury and they expect legal action, but the principals do not believe any action will be taken against them.

At the Fed, the members of the Board will not openly challenge Greenspan, although they may oppose him at their closed meetings. Greenspan's word is *gospel* there; none of them will disobey his order, and any of them will act in his behalf.

I hear at GAO that all the top officials know all of the details and have worked closely together on every action taken in this case, and have approved the actions of the Treasury Department, and Federal Reserve in retaining control of the funds. I hear they know of the Supreme Court Orders to release the funds, charges of collusion and conspiracy, and understand they may be accused of felonious activities in regard to Supreme Court Orders. But, like Rubin and Greenspan, believe nothing will happen to them. I hear they are working to delay audits and reports and turn in incomplete reports whenever they have the opportunity to impede the closure of this deal.

Greenspan is GOD to all these people with regard to banking activities, and no one at GAO, the Fed, Treasury, or any of the banks will act without his approval, and none will take action against him. I hear he has sworn you will never have the funds or any degree of control over any of "his" banks. I also hear he must be either indicted openly or removed from office, and the banking community must be aware of that removal before there can be success. Sealed or suppressed indictments seem to mean nothing to these people. The banks will continue to follow Greenspan's orders—no wall can be built high enough to keep Greenspan from interfering. They may appear to follow Supreme Court orders by moving funds into your accounts and into your payee accounts, but they will not release the funds until Greenspan approves or is removed. It is just unreasonable to them that senior officials of the Fed, the Treasury, the GAO, and Fed Bank officers will be prosecuted. I also hear that if indictments proceed, they intend to bring up a corollary to the "Rostenkowski Argument," which contended the Supreme Court should have no authority to intervene or to order actions against members of the Legislative branch of the Federal Government.

Sincerely,

Jane

March 14, 1995

Dear Mr. Gaus:

I hear that Associate Justices Scalia and Thomas were in Chicago yesterday to make certain there is no misunderstanding about how the Court wishes to proceed. They did set out some rules for the closure.

I hear the agenda at the "rehearsal" includes a plan for warning the banks holding your funds they must take all possible measures to prevent any outsider from gaining control of any of the funds as they are moved to your payee accounts. This includes placing a special watch on each transaction and on each account to thwart any unauthorized payout. Banks on the first, second, and third tiers will be warned they will be held responsible for any funds lost through their accounts. They expect Greenspan to try to pick up the money once you have made payments to your payees. The banks are being advised each payee *must* receive the amount designated by you. Once a payee bank receives funds and safely pays account, the payee bank will be held responsible for the safety and security of the funds.

I hear there is concern a large amount of US dollars suddenly appearing could further devalue the dollar against world currencies. I trust a special message will be (or has been) sent to the payee governments requesting them to take measures to prevent action that might devalue the dollar.

I hear a bill of specific charges against Greenspan is still being drawn up, and he is still working to block the release of your funds.

I hear Mr. Greenspan plans to charge the Supreme Court with pushing to move in a timely fashion because some of them were trying to protect themselves. He is an extremely bitter man who sees himself as being made the scapegoat for Presidents Bush and Clinton, either of whom could have ordered the funds paid out. He will not go quietly.

I hear he feels if the World Bank had been serious about completing the deal, and sure of their position, they should have told it to the media when the Court made its first decision in the case. I hear he knew, from the day Attorney General Reno learned of the matter, he personally contacted the Supreme Court for a full briefing, and then went to the White

House about this, feeling his days were numbered.

I hear his feeling is the World Bank applauded the personal intervention of Attorney General Reno and the Supreme Court and will use this to discredit and destroy Greenspan's reputation; not only with US Banks, but also with banks around the world, so *no* bank will listen to him, nor want to do business with him, and will be extremely reluctant to accept any funds sent by him. I hear Greenspan feels the World Bank now has the upper hand in dealing with world banks, and "all they had to do was hide in their headquarters, be quiet, and let the Supreme Court take me down and destroy all I had built."

March 15, 1995

Dear Mr. Gaus:

The people I talk with do not know much about the details of banking operations. I do not talk with anyone in the Supreme Court, but I talk with people in several other parts of the government. Also, it is difficult to know what the Supreme Court is doing, especially when they want it kept secret, e.g., the list of law violators.

However, I am able to gather some information, which indicates the Court may be considering a funds transfer system for the sole use of First Central Holding Company. The purpose might be to allow the officers of First Central Holding Company to transfer funds in the future without them appearing on the Federal Wire, thus bypassing the Federal Reserve Banks and the holding accounts in those banks. The system might also include a special code for First Central Holding Company funds for use when they are transferred by a Federal Wire. The Court apparently wants to establish a mechanism that will help safeguard your funds from unauthorized entities. They appear to realize the huge amount of money, and the large number of banks under control of First Central Holding Company, demands extraordinary safeguards to provide appropriate security.

Sincerely,<br>Jane

March 18, 1995

Dear Mr. Gaus:

I hear there is much thought going on about the shock to the IRS banking system when First Central Holding Company takes control of a major fraction of the banks. There *is* fear, on the part of some, that FCHC just might close down some of the banks. Others fear FCHC may try to enforce a major house cleaning. Others fear FCHC demands for repayment of sequestered funds would cause failure of many banks and ruin many individual bank officers. The most worrisome fear is that a serious run on the banks might be generated.

The general problem might be eased through the following measures:

1) FCHC agree in writing that no bank will be raided for its assets, nor will any bank be shut down solely as a result of FCHC assuming control. Make it clear to bank officers that:

   a) Trusts of all types, pension funds, foundation accounts, certificates of deposits, accounts of non-profit entities, numerous accounts of all types, and all other funds held by banks as fiduciaries, will not be invaded to pay debt obligations.

b) Gambling in the derivatives market is prohibited.

c) Churning long term Treasury Bond accounts is prohibited.

d) No bank shall create or use Federal Reserve Accounts or any special accounts for the purpose of concealing funds or avoiding reporting requirements.

e) No bank shall engage in using wire transfers to avoid reporting requirements.

f) No bank shall allow any individual to establish a personal or private account for the purpose of avoiding reporting requirements.

2) Remind account holders the FDIC insures them to $100,000 each and point out that FCHC will supplement that up to a total of $250,000 for pre-existing accounts. (Can you stand this?)

3) FCHC establishes a subsidiary corporation that might resemble the now declining Resolution and Trust

Corporation. The objectives of the subsidiary might be to:

a) Negotiate agreements with banks owing monies to FCHC to secure repayment on terms and conditions suitable in each case. Monitor and enforce performance under those agreements.

b) Consolidate loans made by the banks. Classify loans and handle them by type of loan, type of collateral, and quality of borrower.

c) Auction loans to qualified collection and servicing entities. Use proceeds to partially remunerate FCHC with credit to debt of owing paper.

d) Research, negotiate, and prepare litigation to recover funds sequestered by individuals.

e) Support any federal litigation as might be appropriate.

Another problem is the presence of Greenspan, the man who has no friends in Washington. As long as he is in office, the bank officers are going to be extremely reluctant to follow the Court orders, although they know he is wrong. They are afraid (literally) of what he might try to do to them "after the dust settles."

The best solution would be for him to resign for reasons of health, something he will never do. The other solution would be for the US Marshal Service to arrest him under a warrant issued by competent authority (maybe District Court). He has vowed to "never go alone."

I hear he is determined that, if he goes to jail, he wants President Bush in the cell to his left, and President Clinton in the cell to his right.

I hear Greenspan holds signature cards showing Bush and Clinton have opened offshore bank accounts, and deposit reports showing funds deposited in those accounts.

I have been told Bush has been tracking this deal since he was Director of the CIA, and Bush was the mastermind in stealing your money.

I hear Secretary Rubin has been severely shocked over recent revelations to him about this matter. He thought Greenspan was an honorable friend and peer, had no comprehension of the overseas accounts, the disappearance of the funds, formation of offshore corporations for laundering the funds, etc. Now Rubin is being called before the Supreme Court and told he will be arrested if he does not clean up his act. I hear he has told the Court he had no knowledge of the extent of the problem, has no influence *whatsoever* over Greenspan, and has no authority of any kind over him, but, "I'm being told that charges will be brought against me." I hear he told the Court he would testify in support of any prosecution of Greenspan.

I hear Rubin wonders why Clinton does not fire Greenspan and get rid of the problem, but he does not know the extent of the Greenspan/Clinton misdeeds.

I hear the next major headache is the Supreme Court's reluctance to have Greenspan arrested, for then the misdeeds of the Supreme Court would be made public by Greenspan. As I have reported before, they agree unanimously the law of the land must prevail, but they are shocked, angered, and anguished to find that some former members of their august body may have to be prosecuted.

I hear some of those involved at the lower levels are hoping the World Bank officials will press Attorney General Reno to request warrants be issued by the US District Court of Washington, DC, in the event the Supreme Court does not act.

One idea that has come up seems worthy of consideration. As you have pointed out, if you have bucks in the bank, you have the right to write checks to anyone. Following to its logical conclusion, if all your payees had accounts in your designated bank, you could make direct transfers to their accounts without the matter leaving your bank. Only your bank would be in a position to foul the thing up. Such could be arranged by sending signature cards to your payees for execution and return to you. You would then take the cards to your bank, open the accounts, and deposit the funds due to each payee in his/her account. The bank would send checkbooks to the payees who could then transfer the funds piecemeal to the banks of their choice. I believe that the nonresident payees would not incur Illinois State Income Tax liabilities, as they are merely passing the funds through the Illinois bank; however, the advice of an Illinois tax expert might be in order.

Sincerely,
Jane

March 21, 1995

Dear Mr. Gaus:

I hear the offending members of the Supreme Court are frantically searching for *any* remedy to their predicament. It may be too late for them to return the funds which they have accepted, and it is, of course, not likely they will get Greenspan to return the evidence he holds. My sources say the justices do not know how much the World Bank knows about their misfeasance in terms of dates and amounts. I hear the personal horror of destroyed reputations and actual court trial came home to the culprits only when Scalia "preached his sermon" and told them to resign or be exposed. They relied on Greenspan's promises that he could hide the transactions in the banking system so they would never be found. I hear Scalia will not hesitate to make their records public. I hear they have sent the final turnover documents to Chicago but are pleading with Scalia for a "few days" in which to try to raise the funds for restitution, or to find some other way out of their mess.

I hear there is some backdoor trading going on wherein they are going back to

Baker, Brady, and Greenspan for help in repaying the funds, and they have appealed to President Clinton for amnesty. I hear they are being told the Supreme Court should have refused the mess in the beginning. I hear they direct much rage toward the late District Judge Gesell, who first found in favor of the World Bank, and to Scalia, who has forced a sense of legal responsibility on the Supreme Court.

I hear that many legal eagles in Treasury and the White House have been scrambling in search of a way for the president to seize the banks and put them under control of the Fed, or Resolution Trust Corporation. The problem there is they must first show the individual banks are on the verge of failure and that is not the case.

In the past, the president has seized control of the postal system, the rail system, and the air traffic control system, all when the workers went on strike. In all cases there was a clear and present danger to the economy. That situation does not exist in this case; therefore, they cannot use the law that supported those seizures. I hear the Supreme Court told Mr. Rubin there is no legal way in which the turnover can be prevented. Justice Scalia, no doubt, had done his homework before he made that statement.

It is my sense some laws would have to be changed before 1,600 banks could be seized en masse by the government; this is not likely to happen any time soon. Even if the banks could be seized, there would remain the monumental task of explaining to the public and to the world why they were seized. I hear many of the banks are telling the Fed, "We can ride out the effects of this turnover and remain as viable, functioning banks. Seizure would be a horrendous mistake and you should not consider it."

Sincerely,<br>
Jane

March 25, 1995

Dear Mr. Gaus:

I hear the final decision has, in fact, been made and the money, indeed, will be released. I hear Justice Scalia and the Attorney General are working out the legal details and documents to close out this matter. I hear they are determining the language of the public announcement and explanation.

It seems the legal implications may extend to more people than we thought. I hear the Attorney General and Justice Scalia are informing the White House (President Clinton, Leon Panetta, etc.) of their decisions, the legal implications, and the standing of individuals (including Supreme Court justices). I hear they will not stand for any interference or even the attempt of political pressure on any member of the Court. I hear the two justices nominated by President Clinton were called by him, saying that "They should be neutral and not agree to the release of funds as release will bring down my presidency."

I hear Justice Brennon told President Clinton he would not enter into a discussion, as it was most inappropriate. I hear the lady justice, Ruth Bader Ginsberg, is livid with rage and beside herself with fury and delivered a scathing lecture to the president about the impropriety of his talking to her.

I hear she told him that by trying to influence the case, he was committing a felony, and should understand the serious legal implication of any overture to the Court concerning a case before it. I hear she told him he is in serious legal trouble now in other cases, and he should certainly know better than to try to influence any justice.

I hear the Attorney General is deeply saddened this case has come to the point of requiring the Supreme Court, not only to make decisions about a case but having to take it over and actually having to implement their orders, but they must do so due to the failure of the banking system, aided and abetted by the president and other government officials to comply with court orders.

I hear they say the Supreme Court's charter is to interpret the laws and codes in context of the Constitution, and this does not include enforcement of the laws. Now they have an associate justice of the Supreme Court running around with an order in his back pocket, playing the role of a county sheriff.

I hear the attorney general understands President Clinton could not act to release the funds without being destroyed by Greenspan. This may happen anyway, but I hear Attorney General Reno does understand the president is a hostage of Greenspan because of his past misdeeds, both in his home state of Arkansas and in Washington. I hear when all the legal documentation is complete, the attorney general will notify the president and the Senate Banking Committee.

As I said on the telephone, I hear Greenspan is going back to the governments of foreign countries, where he had put your money in the past, and demanded money from the government treasuries, not from the banks. He wants the funds held for him in local currency in accounts, which he will designate. I hear he has demanded $600 million to $700 million from the government of Japan. The questions that might be asked are, "Has he collected any money?" and "How much has he collected?" He is desperate and will try anything.

We wish you a quiet, peaceful Sunday. We will be giving the Lord many hearty "thank you" prayers. He said He would win this battle, and He has won. I know He is looking forward to identifying to us what He wants us to accomplish in His name.

Sincerely,
Jane

March 28, 1995

Dear Mr. Gaus:

We hear the attorney general will carry out her orders, received from the Supreme Court, to the letter. Her actions will be such that they will not be questioned. We hear she has reviewed her orders with her senior staff and has consulted with her division heads. We hear she is charged with drawing up and serving official notices to all parties to the fund's turnover. This will be the official service of the orders of the Supreme Court. The order may include a time window for the turnover, or the time may be set after all have been served. Service will most likely be made by US Marshals to the following:

1) Secretary of the Treasury
2) Controller of the Currency
3) Chairman, Federal Reserve Board
4) Governors of the Federal Reserve
5) President, World Bank, as monitor of the major trust
6) US attorney in each state involved
7) State Banking Authority in each state involved
8) Attorney general in each state involved

9) State Supreme Court in each state involved
10) CEO designated responsible for each bank involved

The US Marshal service in Washington may be called upon to deliver the service documents to the US attorney in each state, who would then use local US Marshals to perform the service.

We hear the Supreme Court wants all of this done during this week. The most likely event is the attorney general will certify to the Court that all required services have been made, whereupon the Court will order the funds released to First Central Holding Company. We hear that, once the Supreme Court is served, if the entity served does not comply, the entity may be charged with contempt and arrested.

Sincerely,
Jane

March 30, 1995

Dear Mr. Gaus:

I hear from my contact the attorney general has not completely finished all the work required by the Supreme Court before they issue a time and date for turnover. She tried to complete the work yesterday, but she got the package late Monday and there is a huge amount of work to do. I hear the orders are out and she is waiting to receive all of the certificates of service. The attorney general has been especially careful to make certain documents are prepared properly, are complete, and are free of grammatical or procedural errors that could sustain a challenge. I hear she has requested a short extension on completion time, so she can be certain everything has been done correctly. She is assembling the warrants and will transmit them for service when the court resolves the timing of their service (before or after release of the funds?).

The Court is aware the World Bank wants the funds released "now." The Court and attorney general are looking at two courses of action. The Court feels the World Bank will not wait much longer. The attorney general feels the warrants should be served simultaneously. I hear they have been working around the clock at Justice since the instructions were delivered.

One of the problems is the Supreme Court took its time preparing the instructions for the attorney general, and then they wanted the job completed immediately. I hear the Supreme Court understands they must have a firm answer ready for the World Bank by close of business, Friday. They feel the World Bank will not, and should not, have to wait any longer. I hear the attorney general will not know, until around noon Friday, when she will have all the services completed; this leaves the warrants and follow up work still to come. The attorney general has made a firm decision that she will not allow "the bad guys" to ruin her reputation.

The Supreme Court justices are still in turmoil—worst case they ever saw—includes one of their own and questions about two others within the Court. There are some frantic people worrying about their futures and are really shattered to understand that they and their official positions have been used to cover up "the boss' lies."

I know it seems like a long time, but the Supreme Court finished with its decisions and instructions only this past weekend, and now they want Justice to complete its part in only four days. I hear the attorney general was really stunned at the enormity of her task—the pure tonnage of paperwork that must be generated and completed in an operation of this scale is completely new to her. As a county prosecutor in Miami, she never saw anything approaching the size of this case. Indeed, it probably is the largest case in the history of the Department of Justice. My contact suggests the World Bank contact the Supreme Court tomorrow afternoon and request a status report and a forecast. My contact says, realistically, it looks like Monday or Tuesday before the Supreme Court and the attorney general can feel secure in releasing the funds, and then turn to the follow-up of legal actions.

Sincerely,

Jane

Alex had regained his strength and was back at work, yet on up through the summer and fall of 1995 the lies continued. Several more bogus window times were given and not executed. Alex continued to persevere, relentless in his fight for what was right. On November 8, he sent the following message to the individuals maintaining positions on the pay order lists:

Everything was completed yesterday and today… All holding banks were instructed and ordered via National Federal Reserve to release inter-bank funds in favor of FCHC and its account holders. All of this was completed via computer systems commencing with N.F.R. system "Monday, last" in New York office of Federal Reserve, and completed in Chicago before noon this date. That leaves only notification and receipting and all other process for final closing and turnover.

NOTE: Also completed was the release, or the request, by Handlers and/ or F.R. for certain people in the banking community to leave, some of which were instructed to leave by today. Greenspan noted that turnover process is in full Go… stating further that the handlers and F.R. personnel having discretion to call me as soon as the Federal Reserve personnel have determined everything is complete. I am to be on constant alert of the turnover notification any minute.

Gaus

Later in the year, Alex received the following fax as word began to spread in the inner circles of "people in the know" around the nation that something big was on the horizon in the world of finance.

Dear Brother, here are some thoughts on your initial copy!

To: THE AMERICAN PEOPLE

FROM: PUBLIC TRUST RESTORATION FOR AMERICA

DATE: December 19, 1995

RELEASE: IMMEDIATE

Be alert for a vital announcement as relates to the US Economy and the National Deficit and Debt.

A US holding company will be making a major tax payment that will significantly impact upon the National Deficit and Debt. Such is the magnitude of this tax payment that it will alter the entire budgetary picture of the US.

Efforts have been made by the government to avoid disclosure of this payment for fear of legal action against those involved. These legal actions range from malfeasance of office to possible treason against the American people!

Expect some initial denial of this report. Further disclosure from this source will follow giving explicit details concerning the above information. Ask your political senators and representatives to press for disclosure on the above.

Three days later, Alex received another interesting fax from his contacts in Washington, confirming that the lid was about to blow concerning a major financial scandal in America:

Moscow/Chicago/Washington
December 21, 1995

Relating to news items Central Research and Investigation, please note the following bulletin: World Bank Chairman and Legal Department have been called to declare full amount of Tax Treaty for payment against National Deficit and National Debt.

World Bank has monitored transactions as relates to general income encompassed in National Holding Company's earnings that generated Tax Treaty. Documentation in file with World Bank and the Holding Company confirm beyond doubt illegal acts committed by players in Washington and elsewhere during the past administration; also, the present administration.

Washington players, and special interest groups, received illegal payments under guise the payments need not be repaid, creating massive fraud against the holding company. More so, parties involved did not declare ill-gotten gains as income and the Internal Revenue Service has not collected taxes on hundreds of millions of dollars. Internal Revenue Service is fully aware of the fraud and has not undertaken action against culpable parties. The US Secretary(s) of the Treasury, commencing with 1989, were fully aware of the illegal payments, did not attempt to collect proportionate taxes from culpable parties. Secretary(s) of the Treasury and others skimmed payments for their personal purposes, not declaring said amounts as required by Tax Law, and have not returned ill-gotten gains to the rightful owner.

Total amount of the Tax Treaty in question, ready for payment now, will wipe out the National Deficit and Debt.

This office and the offices of the World Bank have, in their possession, records noting amounts involved in fraud, dates, persons, parties, banks, etc., and are preparing to publish full disclosure of all materials. The present administration, the past administration, Congress, the Supreme Court of the United States, the Federal Banking Systems, and other government agencies are fully aware of said information and documentation.

Contact Washington; demand your right to the information and the payment of taxes against ill-gotten gains, the crimes committed by Washington, et al., and that Washington cease defrauding the American people.

Gaus

Roger Golden received the following fax from Alex Gaus shortly after the turn of the New Year. As madness was swirling around Washington, an alternate plan was being put in place to bypass the considerable influence of the Chairman of the Federal Reserve, Alan Greenspan.

To: ROGER GOLDEN
FROM: ALEX GAUS
DATE: FEBRUARY 1, 1996
RE: NATIONAL FEDERAL RESERVE

Report from Handler (banker) as of 1600 hours this date: Handler met with N.F.R. and other office in Washington relating to turnover, and the legitimate present status. The questions before the Board of Governors of the fed, concerned certain documents and information/ records that Greenspan withheld from the Board, containing incriminating infor- mation. The whole of the Board is very much concerned about their individual status and well-being because culpability affected all of them (more or less). Also, the Board resolved to wrest the authority from Greenspan and act exclusively as a Board apart from the chairman. The res- olution of the internal strife was resolved (pretty much) by last night with the exception of Greenspan and two members of the Board. [They were overruled.]

Handler noted that because of the turmoil within, the total change in direction became effective today. Also because of the internal change there was some final formulation work to be put in place.

As to timing, Handler noted the turnover details were either being completed as of 1600 EST this date or have been completed as of now. Two fed persons are in Chicago to handle T.O. based on final formulation being (or having been) completed. "Turnover has been scheduled as immediate."

As of 1900 hours, Handler noted further that Greenspan is still creating opposition. However, it does not pertain to the transaction directly but to his own culpable position. Evidently, the Board is acting separately from Greenspan in the turnover process.

We also discovered that Greenspan still has some of our money concealed in accounts, and for him to bring the funds back in compounds his crime.

The Board is also afraid the National Federal Reserve systems will be disbanded.

Gaus

Alex continued to press on with the plan, believing his efforts were not in vain. The following fax was sent to all individuals on the tax treaty, pertaining to the logistics of the dispersal of funds.

To: Coordinate Accounts
FROM: Gaus, FCHC
DATE: February 8, 1996
RE: Release of funds to accounts

PLEASE NOTE: The release of funds for individual accounts is under the tutelage of the U.S. Treasury Department and the United States Supreme Court, represented by the Federal Bureau of Investigation. Authority for the United States Federal Reserve Banking Systems has been removed and the present function of the Federal Reserve is that of "turnover" preparation and necessary clerical work period. All accounts and computer entries pertaining to said accounts are blocked by codes entered in the computer systems by the FBI and an unknown party. Federal Reserve is no longer empowered to freeze the accounts away from the account holders and is not privy to the release codes noted above. Said codes will be disclosed to FCHC today and/or tomorrow and FCHC will be commissioned to push the buttons in company of the FBI and the other unknown entity. Posting of the accounts is thus mechanical and scheduled momentarily. The minute and/or hour of the "button pushing" is unknown "classified" and will not be announced until shortly before the hour. The final setup work for the "button pushing" is in preparation as of this hour 1445 hours, Central Time. Simultaneously, with the account administration will be the turnover of all assets to FCHC, which are part and parcel of the transaction in chief. Accordingly, Federal Reserve cannot dictate as to the posting to coordinate accounts, however, said posting is subject (as noted herein) to button pushing by FCHC.

(Your) bank(s) are still under instruction to notify "their" account holders, however, FCHC will notify account holders of the exact time of "button pushing" and the transfer/posting of receipts. Prior receipts of transfer under alleged authority of Federal Reserve are voided and have expired as to validity.

1450 hours Chicago time, February 8, 1996

Gaus

Talk radio in the nineties had exploded. The Internet was on the horizon, but talk radio was the Twitter of the decade. The American people began to view the mainstream media as being slanted to the left, liberal, and biased. A nationwide tidal wave of outrage had been generated from the grassroots and manifested itself in the form of talk radio. It was an avenue for the people to vent their views and opinions on the latest federal outrage and government scandals.

There was a talk radio show broadcast out of Miami called *We the People*. A significant episode aired on the evening of January 18, 1996, that explained why the Supreme Court was powerless to enforce its own mandates. Alan Greenspan was holding Washington in a state of checkmate by passing out bribes to all those who could not resist to keep them silent—and powerless.

A man named Jay Vincent hosted the show, the contents of which were as follows:

"Computer hackers" uncovered Swiss and offshore accounts in names of congressional and administration persons. An ultimatum was given to such persons to either announce their resignation or their intent not to run for office, within twenty-four hours, or their "brown bag" file (containing bank account information, transaction documentation, etc.) would be released to authorities. Jeff Nelson, a senior editor of *Forbes Magazine*, worked with five rebel hackers at the CIA who had uncovered the foreign accounts and proceeded to bring the funds into a CIA account. Nelson sadly discovered too late one of the board members of *Forbes Magazine*, Casper Weinberger, the former Defense Secretary, had an account as well. Nelson was fired from *Forbes Magazine* upon his attempt to publish the information.

The hackers, who were midlevel CIA employees, had noticed a strange code number attached to the accounts of numerous high-powered Washington players. The code numbers on all the accounts were the same. They became curious and pulled up the accounts, noticing that all of them were offshore or foreign accounts with bogus prefixes. These were the same accounts for which Alan Greenspan had receipts and documentation that he was using to hold hostage individuals who had taken "the bribe."

The names listed on these accounts were incredible; included were presidents, first ladies, first children, and Supreme Court justices, senior senate members, and over forty other members of Congress! Many Bush Administration insiders who made the transition from the Reagan Administration were found to have accounts as well. Corruption through the highest levels of government had spread like a disease, weakening the very moral fiber of the nation. In the era of George Bush's New World Order, there was indeed a new set of rules that ultimately rendered the Constitution itself powerless to stop them.

Before the 1996 elections, a record forty-six Congressman resigned their seats for various reasons. These men and women had mortgaged their eternal future in exchange for ten, twenty, maybe thirty years of the good life—so they thought. It was this successful coup against the United States Constitution that would empower the One-Worlders, known today as the deep state, to brazenly defy the law of the land many times over in the future as the unexecuted Supreme Court order remained sealed in the Supreme Court vault, rendering the High Court powerless to challenge the deep state. The hallowed halls of justice had become irreparably corrupted then and still, to this day, remain so.

Control. Control of power is more important to these people than any amount of money. The entire system of government at the highest levels had broken down. The balance of power—the system designed to keep the three highest levels of the government in check—had been sabotaged by greed. Greenspan had waltzed through Washington, passing out hush money as though it was Halloween and the bigwigs all had a sweet tooth. He was desperate, and there were no rules or no boundaries. Nothing was too unethical in the war he was waging to stay in control.

Never in the history of this nation have so many seats been vacated in one election. Indeed, the system of government upon which America was founded was truly in a state of moral paralysis. The legislative branch could not hold the executive branch in check. The executive branch could not hold the legislative branch in check. Neither the legislative branch nor the executive branch could hold the judicial branch in check, not that they would anyway.

Everyone had dirt on their hands, either because they had taken a bribe or because they were aware of the illegalities taking place in the cover-up and chose to remain silent. National leaders at the highest levels were caught in the vortex of a giant whirlpool of sin, awash in a sea of cover-up and lies. The Supreme Court was powerless to see that their rulings were carried out, because certain members of their prestigious club had compromised their position by accepting hush money. Justice Scalia and Justice Thomas were the good guys, according to the reports Alex had received. But they found themselves in the unenviable position of sending some of their comrades to jail in the process of upholding the law of the land.

Greenspan was rolling the dice. He stated he had received orders "from the top" (Presidents Bush and Clinton) to not release the funds. He knew everyone had dirt on their hands and he held all the cards, extremely confident the odds were in his favor. No one would challenge him without risking their own reputations and careers.

The system of government had broken down. No longer was it the government of the people, by the people, and for the people. The rules had changed—it was now government by the few, the self-serving, the corrupt. A New World Order indeed.

# Hope Deferred

J ust as Pharaoh did, they would stand in defiance until the very end, holding on to the control of the financial empire they had built, along with the hundreds of millions of people they had enslaved to their system. For truly there would be no empire without those enslaved. How many times did Pharaoh stand in defiance of the living God? How many times did Pharaoh say, "Yes, yes, your people can have their freedom?" And then say, "What, do you think I'm stupid? Of course, you can't have your freedom. I am in control of all your people. Your people must do as I say. Why would I want to release them? I am in total control. I am Pharaoh!" Every time Pharaoh promised First to Moses and his people, God knew Pharaoh did not mean what he said. Pharaoh stood in defiance of God with a hardened heart. God was letting Pharaoh hang himself.

There is a strong parallel connecting these two stories, even though thousands of years separate them. How many times was Alex Gaus told "tomorrow"? The origins of this transaction lay in the throne room of God himself. Knowing and understanding that God sees the beginning and the end of the story of mankind, clearly the entire story of "Plan A" has a specific prophetic place in the last days.

The purpose of the entire transaction was not so one man could become the richest man in the world, with wealth in the trillions. Certainly, God had a larger plan in mind when he conceived the strategy. With the premise established that "Plan A" was truly of divine origin, the question begs to be asked, for what purpose? How many times would the leaders of America stand in defiance of the Most-High God? How many times would they say, "Yes, yes, you can have your money tomorrow," all the while knowing they did not speak the Truth? Why would God Almighty allow it to continue? There had to be a larger purpose behind it all.

The men involved in "Plan A" understood that the words written in Scripture contained the essence of life itself. They understood the power of life is in the spoken Word of God. The men in positions of power in this nation were attempting to gain wealth by vanity. Their actions were based on lustful greed and their desire to hold on to vain power.

Alex, Roger, and their families, along with all those involved in the transaction, had experienced personally what it means to have hope deferred, which makes the heart sick, but when the desire comes to pass, they knew it would be as a tree of life. They were confident their God would not allow himself to be mocked or ridiculed by those who lied against the Truth. What a man sows, that shall he also reap.

They knew the wealth obtained by means of vanity would soon be diminished, just as their own efforts would be honored with increase. They continued to call forth into being those things that were not presently in existence, knowing their faith was literally the substance of things hoped for; yet the evidence they could not see with their physical eye. Scripture promises that when the thief is caught, he must repay seven times over that which was stolen! They had no other choice but to take joy in the tribulations they were experiencing.

As their patience was being tested, they remembered seeing the miraculous hand of God deliver them in the past. It was their faith in God that ultimately brought them hope. For years, day after day, they would set their face as a flint, hanging their faith on the words the Spirit of God had spoken to them. They continued to walk by faith and not by sight, for they knew they were guided by divine providence and not by chance. Their expectation was the manifestation of the substance of the things for which they saw by faith.

They continued to persevere, awaiting the day the evidence of their faith would manifest itself in the physical world. Certainly they were all getting a good lesson in patience. It would have been easy for them to give up, but they had made a decision to believe God. They understood God's ways are higher than their ways and His thoughts are higher than their thoughts. So they continued to hope, allowing faith to have its perfect work. They were committed to this journey for the duration, believing God would reveal the details of his purpose and accomplish this thing in his own time. God is never late. However, just as Moses was not allowed to enter the promised land, having served his purpose, the dividing of the promised land among the people as an inheritance belonged to Joshua. The purpose of the Plan-A transaction was yet for a future time and a future purpose.

# What Press Conference?

The two men approached the giant pillars of power as though they were walking up the steps toward the massive marble columns of the Parthenon in Greece. The Chicago skyline stretched powerfully and majestically across the beautiful blue Lake Michigan shoreline, which was itself a pillar, representing the strength of the nation, aptly named the City of Broad Shoulders. Continental Illinois was at one time a pillar amongst the financial institutions of America. Now it was a symbol of the strength of the One-Worlder's evil financial system. It needed to be brought down.

Inside the building, more marble columns extended upward, forming an atrium area. On the walls were large murals containing quotes from great moments in history. Sadly, the structure portrayed the face of evil: beautiful on the outside but corrupt and full of deceit on the inside as they confiscated funds belonging to the American citizenry. Roger and his son, Steve, marched around the building just as Joshua marched around Jericho. Around the columns they went, praying in the spirit and calling upon the Lord of hosts to bring the system to the ground. They had marched squarely into enemy territory, and the activity of the powers of darkness was very real. Yet they confidently marched on, knowing they were surrounded by a mighty invisible angelic host, weapons in hand and ready for battle. Roger and Steve had come to claim their inheritance.

They had flown to Chicago in February of 1997 to meet with Alex for two reasons. Both reasons were strategically offensive in nature. It was time to be aggressive! It was obvious the feds were not going to release the funds voluntarily. They must be challenged legally. Force them to respond to the high-stakes chess game. Force them to make the next move and see how they react. Take the game to them and pressure them into making a mistake. The law was on their side, as is the Most-High God of the universe. Chills ran down Roger's spine as he continued to march. He felt the presence of the Lord of hosts, along with the fullness of his power, as the invisible darkness began to diminish.

The first part of the plan was to give the bank the opportunity to complete the turnover quietly, by walking in and declaring their intentions to assume ownership. If the reception was a chilly one, as was expected, the group was prepared to go forward with a major press conference, openly disclosing the crimes of the conspirators in hopes of avoiding a costly, time-consuming legal battle, of which they held out as a last resort.

Roger, as legal counsel representing the rightful owner, Alex Gaus, was fully intending to take possession of the bank. Alex was prepared to arrive at the bank in a moment's notice if necessary but felt he needed to monitor events from his office to communicate with his insider connections: Sue Swank and her close friend inside the bank, and his old friend Jane in Washington at Treasury. Roger and Steve met the receptionist and a chain of other individuals en route to a meeting with the senior vice president of the bank, Robert F. Coleman, who was an individual fired for his misdeeds of the Continental Illinois days and later rehired under Bank of America. Alex would later learn it was Coleman who was one of the key players funneling funds through BankAmerica in San Francisco. BankAmerica, of course, illegally purchased Continental Illinois from the FDIC after Continental Illinois had been sold to First Central Holding Company as part of the turnover plan from the illegally seized funds.

Coleman coolly ushered them into his office. They wanted to press him into a corner and see how he reacted. Roger lay down copies of Alex's holdings in the bank, in accordance with the numerous concessions, tax treaties, and other various documents Alex had provided. He told Coleman he was in the bank as legal representative to the rightful owner, Alex Gaus, and was there for the purpose of assuming ownership.

Before receiving Roger and Steve into his office, Coleman had instructed his staff to alert their superiors of First Central's presence in the bank. The strategic move of an unannounced appearance at the bank undoubtedly caught the hierarchy of the power structure off guard. The phone lines were busy from Chicago to Washington, across the street at the feds building; at the Department of Treasury, Justice, the Federal Reserve, and the White House. The network of communication amongst the powers that be was active with one theme: "Gaus's attorney is in the bank to take possession!"

Like rats in their subterranean network, players on all levels were scurrying around trying to decide how to handle the unexpected appearance of Roger Golden in the bank. Stone-faced and expressionless on the outside, Coleman could not wait for this day to be over. This was the last thing he expected to have to deal with when he woke up. Deep inside his spirit, where deep speaks to deep, Coleman knew he would have to, once again, lie against the Truth. Try to change it and contort it. He knew one day he would have to stand before Truth and give account of his actions. But that day was too far off to matter. What mattered to him now was surviving in the system of lies and cover-up, created by individuals loyal to the father of lies. Coleman knew what he was about to do was wrong, but he was in too deep.

Coleman denied all knowledge of the deal and said little in response to the questions asked. Roger made it clear he was aware Coleman knew what was going on. It was at that point Coleman excused himself and left the office. Roger presumed he was going to call his boss for advice as to the events currently taking place, so Roger decided to do the same.

While sitting in the office of the vice president of the bogus Bank of America, Roger called Alex. Before he could even get a word out, Alex informed Roger his contacts in Treasury had just confirmed Roger and Steve were in the bank, while they were still there! That alone proved the existence of the legal position of First Central, and the existence of the cover-up.

Coleman returned to his office a few minutes later and said curtly, "My apologies, gentlemen. Now, was there going to be anything else?"

Roger knew he had Coleman in a corner now and decided to press the issue. "So let me understand you correctly. You're going to sit face-to-face across from the representative of the rightful owner of Continental Illinois, with a file full of supporting documentation, and continue to deny the existence of the legal position of First Central Holding Company. Is that correct?"

Coleman said, "I'm afraid I still don't know what you're talking about."

"Well, then," said Roger, "let me rephrase the question. Are you going to continue to play the role of the good little puppet of the One-Worlders and lie against the Truth? I find it very interesting that just after you let the rest of your One-Worlder cronies know First Central was in the bank to assume ownership, our people were calling us to let us know the One-Worlders in Washington were now aware of our presence in the bank. So what I want to know is, if you have no idea who First Central Holding Company is, why did you feel you had to call your bosses in Washington to tell them First Central Holding Company was in the bank? I'm guessing you were scared, maybe even shocked and didn't know what to do. Am I right?"

The blood immediately began to rush to the face of Robert F. Coleman as he stood up and said, "I'm afraid I'm going to have to ask you to leave now."

"It's all right," said Roger, "you don't have to answer. It's obvious what is going on here." Roger and Steve stood up, and then Roger said something he later wished he hadn't. "We came prepared to discuss business in a civil manner, but since you continue to deny the truth, we are left with no other option but to follow through with our plans to carry on a press conference to reveal the truth to the American public of crimes committed against not only First Central Holding Company but also against the American citizenry over the past eight years. Just in case you decide you would prefer to stay out of jail and discuss things between now and then, here is my card. Feel free to call me. I'm sure you can work out a deal for your own immunity."

As Roger and Steve headed down to their car, Alex called Roger and said, "So how did it go?"

"Well, I guess it got a little heated at the end, I'm sorry to say," said Roger.

"Why are you sorry?" Alex said, laughing. "Those guys need a little fire under their ass! I am anxious to hear all about it."

Steve was Roger's chauffeur as well as legal assistant. He opened the trunk to the dark-green Lincoln and loaded the briefcases, opened the door for his father, and jumped in the other side. Not only was he excited to be there, joining in the fight, but he was also beaming with pride for his dad. As he pulled out of the parking garage, turning left onto Jackson Street, he said, "So where are we going?"

Roger said, "Turn left up here onto Lakeshore Drive and follow it around for a few miles. We are meeting Alex for dinner at the Navy Pier."

The two reflected on the events of the day as they traveled along the waterfront of Lake Michigan. Steve saw the mighty white caps crashing into shore and he remembered the times Roger had brought them to Chicago when they were kids. He said, "Some of my favorite memories were with you and Mom and Greg and Rich running around all of the different cultural museums on the lakefront. Those were special times."

A wave of emotion began to rise up inside of Steve as he said to his father, "Dad, I just want you to know something. I want you to know how proud I am of you. I could not ask for a better father! Whether we are running around science museums or doing battle with the evil money gods…I mean, I was watching you in Coleman's office. I was so proud of you. No, we did not come out of there with the bank papers in our hands, but we did something significant in there today. Along with rattling the gates of hell, we looked the powers of darkness in the eye and stood up for what was right. We fought for the liberation of the Truth today and it felt great! It's an honor to be your son."

There was a brief pause, and Steve glanced over at Roger to see him looking straight ahead, his bottom lip quivering and a rogue tear inching down his cheek. Steve began to get choked up as well, but just continued to drive.

After taking a deep breath and slowly letting it out, Roger said, "You have no idea how much that means to me, Steve. All the money in the world could not buy what you just gave to me. You just made it all worth it. Even so, it has been a long time waiting for this deal to finish. After a decade of playing fair and waiting, a roller coaster decade full of empty promises—always tomorrow, tomorrow, tomorrow—now it is time for phase two of the plan. All we ever wanted was what rightfully belonged to us. But, the financial-political power structure, including elected leaders at the highest levels, have illegally denied us that right. So now we go public. It's time to expose them for who they really are."

Suddenly they came upon the Navy Pier, and Roger said, "Just up here on the right."

"Right here?"

"Affirmative!" Roger said as if he were suddenly back in command of his P-2V patrol plane. No matter if Roger was riding in a golf cart to the next tee or flying over the Caribbean, he was trained to give directions and give directions he did well.

As they quickly headed inside to get out of the bitter lakefront windchill, the waitress greeted them. Roger said, "We're meeting a gentleman. Alex Gaus is his name."

"Ah, yes," she replied. "Mr. Gaus has arrived, and we have reserved a special table for you. Right this way, please."

They followed the waitress through the large lower level of Riva, which also had a spacious patio area enclosed for the winter. Designer tiled floors stretched from one end to the other, and massive mahogany woodwork lined the walls to the ceilings. Steve was particularly impressed with the large wooden tall-mast sailing ships, which provided the appropriate maritime ambiance. They were led up the stairs to the white tablecloths of the second level, around the corner to a private room overlooking the harbor entrance to the marina where Alex Gaus sat smiling, awaiting their arrival.

Alex stood up to greet his friends, and Steve said, "I believe you picked the right place, Alex. I can only hope the food is as spectacular as the view."

Alex smiled. "I don't think you'll be disappointed." He then looked at Roger, who had picked up the bottle of '93 vintage Quintessa sitting in the middle of the table, and said, "I thought I should show you some love. I mean who leaves Florida for Chicago in the middle of February?"

"I can't argue with that," said Roger as Alex began to pour the classic wine into everyone's glass. "Excellent choice in wine, my friend," Roger said.

"Thank you very much, sir," Alex responded.

As Steve looked out the window overlooking the water, which was barely visible behind the white tops of the sleek yachts that lined the pier, he was fixated on the view of the powerful financial district where they had just spent the afternoon. The glass towers, now gleaming with the rays of the setting sun in the background, represented the very forces against which they struggled. In a moment of inspiration, Steve then raised his glass and said, "And here's to our forthcoming victory on the horizon!"

"To victory!" his older mentors chimed in as the sound of their glasses was heard once again.

Alex said, "You know, the authors of the Constitution of the United States of America and the Declaration of Independence were divinely inspired by biblical laws and principles. God created mankind to be freewill entities and God created man, above all else, for fellowship. His desire was that mankind would freely interact in a relationship of love and intimacy with him. It was not his desire that men be robots or slaves but that they would see God in his love and mercy and freely return the affection. Ultimately, those who learn to do this on their own, in this temporal life, with blinders on their eyes prohibiting them from seeing God as he really is—those are the ones who will please God. Without faith, you cannot please God. Faith is the substance of things hoped for, the evidence of things not seen. This nation is strong because freedom, allowed to flourish within the boundaries of justice and equity, pulls from the resources within all men. This provides all people the opportunity to fulfill their potential dreams and desires."

Roger said, "That reminds me of what is carved above the entrance to the City Hall building in downtown Detroit. Above the statue of Atlas holding the world on his shoulders is the following inscription…"

Steve interrupted him. "'And the Lord is that spirit, and where the Spirit of the Lord is, there is liberty.'"

Roger looked at Steve with a smile on his face and said, "That verse of Scripture on the City Hall building was carved in an era when men understood the correlation between the success of America and biblical principles upon which this great nation was founded. Think about that statement. *Where the Spirit of the Lord is, there is liberty.* If the Spirit of the Lord is where liberty is, then liberty cannot exist apart from the Spirit of the Lord. The correlation between the gradual removal of God from public institutions and the diminishing state of liberties is not accidental.

"Nowhere in the Constitution do you find the statement 'separation of church and state.' However, you do find the government ordered to stay out of the subject of religion entirely. The government is required not to prohibit the free exercise of religion and not to condone one religion as being the 'official' religion. Religion is a subject the Constitution deems off-limits to the government. That is one of the great tragedies of the modern age, the twisting of the constitutional directives toward the government with regards to the subject of religion. Satan's biggest trick is to mix just a little bit of deceit in with the Truth. Just as he did with Eve in the beginning, tricking her with his subtlety and twisting God's words. So it is with the term 'separation of church and state.' It does not exist in the Constitution."

Alex added, "For the majority of the twentieth century, America has been on a level of superiority, relative to other nations, based on wealth, freedom, military power, and belief in 'justice for all.' The objective of the globalist community is to have a system in which all nations are on the same equal level. This is necessary for their One-World policies to be put in place. If the United States exists on a level of superiority to the rest of the nations of the world, the system of One World Government will not work. Therefore, their strategy is to weaken America to 'level the playing field.' It would be necessary to weaken the foundation the nation was built upon in order to weaken the nation itself, diminishing personal liberties and attempting to remove God from society, implementing giant government red tape, and the weakening the military.

"Why, when the technology existed in the early eighties, did the military not build an antimissile defense system? One of the few specific mandates the government is given in the Constitution is the creation, funding, and operation of a military force to *defend* the land. Since the early seventies, the leaders of this nation have adhered to policies that do not make any sense. They have abided by treaties with nations, the Soviet Union for example, that are not in the best interest of the American people. The leaders signed a treaty and still abide by it, even though the nation they signed it with no longer exists. This treaty commits the US to not build a system that will defend itself against incoming missiles! How much common sense does it take to figure out that defending this nation, with available technology against incoming missiles, might be important?

"This policy is in direct violation of the Constitution and is nothing short of treason. Only recently has there been talk of trying to reverse this policy, but will it be in time? Now, China has all of America's nuclear secrets. How they obtained those secrets is nothing short of treason. Now there is no system in place to defend American citizens from this threat. Not only from China but also North Korea. This is an example of the One-Worlder elite sacrificing the good of the nation for their globalist goals. They are intent on weakening the United States to even the playing field before they implement their One World systems.

"Furthermore, the framers of the Constitution were also extremely specific about the creation of money. Article 1, Section 8 clearly states that Congress, the representative body for the people, is charged with the 'power to coin money and regulate the value thereof.' Originally, the states were required to authorize only gold or silver as payment for debts. The life of a nation is controlled by the power to create money and regulate its quantity and value. Therefore, the creation of the Federal Reserve in 1913 was a huge priority to the One-Worlders. By controlling the creation of money and the regulation thereof, the Federal Reserve has effectively assumed control of the nation. By controlling money, the rulers of the feds have it within their power to create economic conditions that can make or break political leaders.

"Most people credit or blame their political leaders for the economic conditions during their tenure in office. The One-Worlders understand if the Federal Reserve has the power to create money and to create economic climates, they have removed these powers from the leaders of the nation and, thusly, removed the democratic control from the people. The Federal Reserve is a private corporation. Major banks own its stock. Major banks are owned and run by One-Worlders."

Alex looked across the table at Roger and Steve and by the look on their faces he could tell they were enjoying the conversation. Alex winked at Steve, who was the only individual at the table from the younger generation; Alex knew Steve would cherish this experience as one to remember.

Alex calmly took a sip of his wine before continuing to share his insights. "The majority of the founding fathers were against the formation of a Central Bank for the United States. In fact, only Alexander Hamilton was a proponent of the issue. Thomas Jefferson referred to a private, central bank, such as National Federal Reserve, controlling the issuing of currency to the public as being 'a greater menace to liberties of the people than any standing army.' This is the author of the Declaration of Independence stating that the Federal Reserve Bank is of more danger to the personal liberties of Americans than the invasion of American shores by a foreign army! Yet, today, the chairman of the Federal Reserve can alter the economic flow to millions of people, billions of dollars, with a five-minute press conference.

"Since the origin of this nation, the Illuminati One-Worlders have fought for the creation of a Central Bank to take the power to create money out of the hands of the people. They were fought and defeated every step of the way by the founding fathers of this nation and those who understood it to be their responsibility to lead by the same principles.

"The success of the One-Worlders' attempt to create a Central Bank, privately owned by them, which would in effect bypass the political power of the nation, truly means the loss of liberty for all Americans. The president would select the chairman and the members of the board of the Fed, but they would serve terms much longer than that of the president, thus giving them power out of the president's reach. The compound interest the Central Bank would charge on money created from nothing would quickly multiply into staggeringly large amounts of money.

"They would get their claws into the giant corporate world as well, especially the media. By extending large lines of credit, catering to all of the executive's needs, including exorbitant personal accounts, the One-Worlders would essentially create the lifeblood of the operations of the large corporations and, with that, carry the ability to dictate policy. For example, a major media corporation is on the verge of releasing a story damaging to the Federal Reserve or the hierarchy thereof. With the threat of calling in debt, thus causing potentially huge problems for the company and the executives, the story is immediately scrapped."

Steve interjected a question. "I wonder if the One-Worlders will have an impact on our press conference? I wonder if they know about it yet?"

Roger smiled and said, "Oh, you can believe *they know.* If you recall, I mentioned it in Coleman's office. It will be interesting to see how it plays out."

Steve said, "How did the major banks get away with securing these loans to underdeveloped nations by American taxpayer dollars?"

Alex shrugged his shoulders and took a deep breath. "I know where you're going with this and I know how you feel. The major banks, with the assistance of the Fed, get their loans secured as a safety net in the form of the American taxpayer. Any loans made in poor judgment will ultimately be paid back by the American taxpayer. For example, the billions of dollars loaned to Brazil, which they most likely will be unable to repay. But the major banks, of course, will still get the profits from the interest. These problems will never go away unless the Federal Reserve act is repealed. In 1913, there was no income tax, and the federal debt was near zero. In 1990, the federal debt was over $3 billion, and the income tax system was incredibly out of control. Now, seven years later, the federal debt is almost $5 billion. Where will it be ten years from now? They will just keep printing money out of thin air as the dollar gets weaker and weaker until the entire deck of cards collapses."

Alex continued, "The grand scheme designed by the One-Worlders is to control the flow of money in this nation, from the unconstitutional origins of the Fed, through the confiscation of all gold bullion during the Great Depression and the dismantling of the gold standard in 1972, to the fabricated Black Monday, costing investors billions just to perform a test run for future events. Now they have illegally seized funds rightfully belonging to First Central Holding Company. This nation truly is perilously on the brink of allowing the foundations upon which it was formed to not only crumble from beneath but to be done so intentionally by a silent assassin in the form of the National Federal Reserve Corporation, a giant tentacle of the Globalist One-Worlders. A prominent member of the Illuminati, I believe it was J. P. Morgan, once said, 'If the American people knew what was really going on, there would be a revolution tomorrow.'"

Roger said, "The quote that stood out in my mind was the Thomas Jefferson quote… Public currency issued by a private Central Bank was 'a greater menace to the liberties of people than a standing army on our shores.' The Feds are the standing army!"

Steve then said, "I also find it interesting to note the strength of the National Federal Reserve Corp, while being privately held, affords ownership to an elite group of One-Worlders, which also may very well be their Achilles' heel, legally speaking."

"I see your point, Steve," Alex said. "We may have to act on that insight in the future." With that, their entrées arrived.

Alex decided to change the subject. "So, Roger, do you think we can count on Barber Conable's support publicly when things start to get a little crazy? I mean, we don't want to make him feel uncomfortable, but certainly his name adds credibility to the story."

Roger said, "His nephew Vic told me he said, 'Try to keep my name out of it if possible. I hate the blasted media! I am certainly not going to lie to them. But you must understand—I walk a delicate line between the world of true patriots, such as yourselves, and those whom you refer to as One-Worlders. My trick is to balance both worlds without sacrificing access to either. It is not an easy thing to do. You can use my name but keep the media away from me. You are as far as my name goes, fair enough?' Vic said he agreed, so we will take our chances. We certainly do not want to burn any bridges."

After their feast, it was back to the war room where the brain trust was formed to devise the plan of attack. Involved in the group were Alex Gaus, Roger Golden, Steve Golden, and DeMarco Baily. DeMarco was a confidant of Alex's for many years. His area of expertise was his media contacts, though not mainstream, and he also wrote for the *London Sunday Times*. Steve would later learn DeMarco was a rogue plant of the One-Worlders, a double agent sent as an insider to earn Alex's trust while keeping his masters apprised of Alex's every move.

The purpose of the assembly of the group was the creation of the press release, the list of media contacts invited to the press conference, and the details of follow-up.

They worked diligently on the project over the next two weeks. The chemistry of the group was tight. Alex and Roger were like best friends, enjoying the strange brand of humor they displayed with each other by doing character imitations and telling jokes from TV shows such as *Laugh-In*. Even in all his frailty of health, Alex's favorite pastime was flirting with the waitresses when they went out to eat. Alex greatly enjoyed the times he spent with Roger, as his family was not intimately involved in the project with him. Alex's sons felt somewhat as though the whole thing was "pie in the sky," making the time spent by the group together even more treasured in Alex's eyes.

The previous summer, Roger had gone through a bout with lymphoma cancer and subsequent chemotherapy treatments. Alex had been in and out of the hospital a half dozen times over the previous couple of years. He was required to use a catheter, and the doctors told him his heart was operating at about 10 percent of its capacity. Both men, playing the role of old grizzled war heroes, knew their days were numbered.

The trip to Chicago was a shining moment in the entirety of the battle. They both knew the purpose was so lofty, they felt as if they were on the front lines of the war, doing battle in the trenches against an adversary who identified himself through his reluctance and silence, stone-faced in his message: "Who are you to approach me, the Money God?" Who has such tentacles spread throughout the world?

Yet there they were, the dragon slayers, poised to take down the mighty empire. Steve felt like the young knight on the royal quest with the battle-hardened warriors and he was honored to be a part of the fight.

There were over twenty-five major and local media outlets on the list. The following is a copy of the notice that went out:

February 1997
RELEASE: IMMEDIATE

SHOCKING!

On Friday, Feb. 14, 1997, at 2:00 PM CST, the *legitimate owner* of BankAmerica, (including the former Continental Illinois Bank), Mr. Alex Gaus, Jr., Trust Manager for First Central Holding Company, Inc., will hold a major press conference on the steps of the former Continental Illinois Bank, now known as BankAmerica, at the corner of Johnson and Lanier Streets, Chicago IL.

FRAUD

Mr. Gaus and legal counsel for First Central Holding Company, Inc., are prepared to reveal factual information and documentation which, in their opinion, discloses *major fraud (including stock fraud), conspiracy, malfeasance, misfeasance and nonfeasance of office* at the highest levels of the federal and state governments, involving past and present administrations.

## FINANCIAL COMMUNITY INVOLVED

Involved (and fully knowledgeable) in all aspects of the case are the United States Supreme Court, the US Treasury Department, ...the Federal Reserve, other major agencies of the government community, and major political names in the executive branch and Congress. Democrat, Republican, past and present.

## WORLD BANK

The World Bank (and former chairman, Barber Conable) and the legal department thereof, have been active for some time in an effort to stymie the rampant impropriety's relating to said federal agencies and the American financial community, and to restore and transfer bona fide tax dollars to the United States government.

## WELL-KNOWN PEOPLE IMPLICATED

First Central Holding Company, Inc., (its) Trustee Board, Alex Gaus Jr., and legal counsel for First Central Holding

Company, Inc., have been reluctant to take this step, but now, confronted with continued refusal by the government to turn over First Central's properties, have no alternative but to reveal documentation which will implicate some of the most allegedly respected persons in the United States today. Documentation in the files of First Central Holding Company, Inc., and the World Bank offices will likely shock the American people.

ISSUED BY:
Alex Gaus, Jr.
Roger Golden, Attorney at Law
First Central Holding Company, Inc.

The following is a copy of the speech Roger had prepared for the press conference:

We have been involved in this case for the past decade, and in our opinion, if ever there were grounds for impeachment proceedings against the Supreme Court of United States and the president, this could very well be it.

*Congress, be alert!*

Our monies arrived in the US in the normal course of business; custody and control were seized by the government.

Early in our negotiations with the government for the recovery of the property of Mr. Gaus, an agreement with the government was reached for the purchase, by Mr. Gaus, of Continental Illinois Bank for the amount of $4.5 billion. This amount was duly paid, but the government has, to this date, failed to deliver ownership. The issue was clouded a few years ago by the disclosure of BankAmerica's (alleged) acquisition of Continental Illinois Bank. To the best of our information, BankAmerica has not yet paid the government for this acquisition, and further information discloses their indebtedness to Mr. Gaus as being in excess of their net worth!

We stand here today in good faith, minute by minute requesting the return of his properties to Mr. Gaus. We have dealt with the government in good faith. We have not established any offshore accounts. We consider ourselves Americans first. We have negotiated a tax treaty with the government. We have agreed to pay the government's assessment of those taxes. And the government has made it impossible to do so.

Several years ago, in reaction to continued governmental delays, Mr. Gaus, in conjunction with the World Bank Legal

Department, and former Chairman, Barber Conable, filed a writ of mandamus complaint with Judge Gerhard Gesell of the D.C. Federal Court, who issued a mandate whereby the government would be ordered, by the court, to do those things it was legally obligated to do: To wit—turn over and give possession of his properties to Mr. Gaus.

Subsequently, on Wednesday, October 7, 1992, the Supreme Court of United States issued its order in an affirmative response to this writ. But no such turnover has yet taken place. We now direct your attention to the official files in the Supreme Court and strongly urge you to investigate and validate this for yourselves. In addition, Mr. Barber Conable has asked us to tell you he will accept accredited members of the press only, who have been established with us first, to view documents in his possession which support the position of Mr. Gaus. Will those of you who wish this accreditation be sure to see me at the conclusion of this conference. A list of your names will be sent to Mr. Conable and you will be notified accordingly.

OUR OBJECTIVES

157

1. We ask, again, for the turnover to Mr. Gaus of his properties. These properties have been lodged for "safekeeping" with BankAmerica, Chicago Branch.

2. We have been involved in face-to-face discussions for some time with BankAmerica—they have not denied our claim. We ask them again, "Please turn over our property!" whether by the execution of the court order or by the voluntary action of BankAmerica.

3. A paramount benefit of this turnover will be the payment of tax dollars to the American people, which have been unreasonably withheld for the last decade. Had these taxes been collected in the beginning, the budget deficits, as well as the national debt would have been effectively wiped out.

4. Finally, this will allow Mr. Gaus and many other persons to commence the doing of the Lord's work—as best we understand His guidance and His will! Malice and revenge are not in our vocabulary. We invite anyone with knowledge and information to please step forward and assist us in any way possible on behalf of the American people.

Thank you, ladies and gentlemen.

The following communiqués were sent out to the twenty-five media outlets who committed to attend the press conference, as well as numerous prominent religious figures around the nation.

Attention: News Director / Editor
News reporters
Release immediate
February 1997

To those who responded in the affirmative to attend our press conference on February 14, 1997, at 2:00 PM CST at BankAmerica, Chicago, on "The Scandal of Modern Times," we have provided some information for you to investigate prior to the date, which will allow you to process the information more efficiently, as the amount of information can be quite daunting at first glance.

We understand that, as members of the press, you are investigators. We ask you not *prejudge us* without *full investigation* of our claims. We believe this is not so! We realize our story is different and unusual and we know it deserves to be told!

To the best of our knowledge and information, a major aspect of our claims now centers around the former Continental

Illinois Bank, now BankAmerica, Chicago Branch.

We indicated there have been improprieties in the past. As far as we are concerned, we look directly to 1991, when the government (FDIC) sold its ownership position of Continental Illinois Bank to First Central Holding Company, then refused to turn over the assets!

These wrongdoings still exist today! We have been direct and truthful in this matter.

We would also like you to know that we have been in face-to-face discussions with bank officers of BankAmerica regarding our claims, and therefore speak with credibility! Please accept our invitation and find out for yourselves what has occurred and is continuing to this day.

In our initial release, we stated that prominent people are either aware or involved but as yet have not seen fit to co mment or act upon our behalf, as we believed they would! It is well known by us all that money, especially *large* amounts, can change people like almost nothing else!

Extend us professional courtesy and investigate our claims. Do not prejudge us or this story! It has refused to die, and it

must be told and, even more, *investigated!*
(Page 1 of 2)

We ask you to investigate this issue
with the following statements and questions, which are further stated to the best
of our knowledge, information, and belief:

Initially, funds earned by Mr. Gaus
arrived from abroad on July 30, 1989,
in Morgan Guaranty Bank, New York.
The funds were destined for his accounts,
then in place at Standard Charter Bank of
Chicago, but never reached them.

1. An exceptionally large input of funds
   was sent to North Carolina National
   Bank (which became NationsBank) in
   the latter part of 1989 and the early
   part of 1990 to "Special Accounts."

2. There are some who would assume
   Continental Illinois Bank was never
   sold by the government (FDIC) to
   First Central Holding Company in
   1991. Has it been assumed that there
   is no record of the sale of Continental
   Illinois to First Central Holding
   Company?

3. Did BankAmerica and the government (FDIC) work together to hide
   the fact of the sale of Continental

Illinois Bank to First Central Holding Co.?

4. Should not all documents relating to the sale of Continental Illinois Bank by the government in 1991 be examined, as they may relate to the sale of Continental Illinois Bank to BankAmerica in 1995?

5. Should not the law firms, individuals, and officials of BankAmerica and the FDIC be interviewed pertaining to this acquisition and the documents reviewed?

6. *Does BankAmerica have anything to hide? If not, then we are sure they will cooperate fully!*

7. Why has the United States Supreme Court not enforced their own order issued on October 7, 1992, to return to Mr. Gaus his properties, pursuant to a writ of mandamus? This order was sent to all Appeals Courts, District Courts, the World Bank and, the Federal Reserve System.

Obtain proof of our claims for your own investigations of BankAmerica and others as mentioned in our questions and statements. We will continue relentlessly to seek return of the properties belonging to Mr. Gaus, presently under the custody and control of BankAmerica. We invite BankAmerica to continue our discussions to resolve this situation. At some point, integrity and common sense must prevail. All future interviews may be scheduled on the condition that there has been personal investigation of this case, pursuing answers to the above questions. Such interviews will be conducted in private.

The following communiqué was sent to the various religious leaders around the nation:

*First Central Holding Co., Inc.*
*Alex Gaus, Jr.*
Re: Government and financial community malfeasance, nonfeasance, and misfeasance.

We come to you in all sincerity and with full belief and faith in our Lord and Savior, Jesus Christ, knowing the same Holy Spirit guides you as well as ourselves. We pray you will give this communication your complete attention and objective scrutiny.

This matter concerns the misuse and abuse of power within the government of the United States and our financial community. Enclosures are attached hereto and made a part hereof (press conference material), intended to provide a summary background for you of this case.

Briefly, our government and financial community have refused to turn over our properties, which came into this country in the course of legitimate business activities on July 30, 1989, and have been misappropriated and withheld from us to this day, in spite of our continuing good faith efforts to negotiate a turnover.

Accordingly, pursuant to our prayers and efforts to seek and understand the Lord's guidance, we felt it was necessary to apprise the country of the situation in order to put pressure on the government and financial community to perfect our turnover, as they were legally required to do. The attached enclosures disclose our efforts.

We notified BankAmerica early of our intentions to hold a press conference which would relate our case to the world, thereby allowing them an additional twenty-four hours within which to voluntarily, and reasonably, turnover and return our properties. We then sent out invitations to various major and lesser media sources to attend our press conference, out of which we had six positive responses, fifteen possible, and only two negatives.

We believe our properties to be of the Lord and for the Lord. We believe the arrogance and corruption in high places to be of the adversary and subject to the Lord's program to cleanse and restore America to the paths of righteousness upon which it was founded.

Further, we believe the package we are now able to present to you was divinely inspired. Our impartiality, sincerity, objectivity, and integrity should be readily apparent.

Lastly, in further response to our prayers, we seek your cooperation and assistance in accomplishing the return of our assets. As we stated previously, it is the conviction of our spirit that these properties are of the Lord and should be utilized in accordance with his will and for his glory. This is truly an opportunity in the end times to see the Lord's properties returned to the rightful owner.

We are sending this letter to many outstanding Christian personages. Setting aside all chances for personal aggrandizement, this is truly a divinely inspired opportunity for all Christendom to unite to defeat the adversary and to do the Lord's work and will, all to his glory!

We, respectfully then, implore you to sit together with us, explore the facts of the case, pray for the Lord's guidance, and determine his plan of action.

Time is of the utmost essence.

May God's blessings be with you,

Alex Gaus, Jr.

Sue Swank, Alex's mole contact at the bank via her friend, was trying to figure out what was going on as well. She was exposed to daily information regarding numbers and figures of the account balance of First Central Holding Company, as well as the parade of bigwigs in and out of the bank. The following fax from Sue Swank to Alex is indicative of the two-faced game the One-Worlders were playing. They knew Alex had the ability to monitor his account, so they had to give the appearance of credibility to their illegal operation.

Here is the message from the mole:

> The Indians here are wondering if in fact the treaty documents are all in, what is the holdup? If the proper people are in the reservation, what can be done to speed up the peace pipe? I would sure hate it if someone got scalped as a result of your upcoming press conference. They are ready for a face-to-face meeting. Please advise. We would also like to know who the Chief would be and how to get to that person.

Roger's youngest son, Rich, called him the morning of the news conference and said, "Good morning, Dad!"

"Good morning, my son!" said Roger. "To what do I owe the pleasure?"

"Well, first, I wanted to tell you I've been praying for you and I want you to know you have the full support of the kingdom of heaven behind you, so be of good cheer! I also wanted you to know I had the strangest dream last night. I think the Holy Spirit is trying to tell us to rest in his peace and know he has everything under control. Still, it was a strange dream in a positive way, so I wanted you to hear about it before your day got under way. As soon as I awakened from the dream, I grabbed my notebook and wrote down as many details as I could remember while it was fresh on my mind, so bear with me as I read you what I wrote."

Roger, not knowing what to expect, said, "Okay, I'm all ears!"

Rich said, "A dream within a dream unfolded in front of me, and I was a silent observer. A brilliant, translucent light silently exploded into the darkness as the angel of the Lord appeared in the middle of the night in the bedroom of Justice Clarence Thomas. The judge, startled and confused, pulled the covers up over his head in fear. The dark room was overwhelmingly brightened by the illuminating presence of the heavenly creature, who stood over ten feet tall. His bronze skin glistened under the brilliant white robe covering his ripped body bulging with muscles. He had long flowing blond hair, which touched the top of his massive shield draped over his back. His mighty sword hung from his belt and glowed from the giant golden handle to the silver, transparent, razor-sharp point at the tip of the blade, which matched the color of the shiny bands of angelic steel wrapped around his huge biceps.

"Thomas panicked as he cried out, 'Who are you! What do you want?'

"The angel said, 'I am Arrikahn, a messenger and fellow servant of the Lord of hosts, King Jesus, the Creator of all thigs. Your presence has been requested before the Great and Merciful Judge, the Most-High God of the Universe! Come, there is much to see.' Suddenly, the earthly bondages of restraint were powerless, as Thomas and his angelic guide were flying freely through a mysterious tunnel of bright light.

"The light grew brighter and brighter the farther they went. They reached the end of the tunnel, and all darkness disappeared completely. The light was brighter than any Thomas had ever seen. Time seemed to no longer be relevant, eternal yet instantaneously nonexistent. Thomas was now traveling through another dimension. They arrived in a giant hall, the size of which was beyond measure. The magnificent beauty of the place was stunning! Thomas found himself in awe of the wondrous glory that emanated from the center of the endless great hall and seemed to be the source of light for the entire heavenly realm. He thought, *What is the great light?*

"Arrikahn answered, 'That is the throne of the Living God.'

"'How did you know what I was thinking?' Thomas asked.

"'Verbal speech is not necessary here. Of course, you may still use it if you wish,' the angel said.

"'Where are we going?' Thomas asked.

"'You will soon see,' Arrikahn said.

"Thomas found himself in the presence of countless thousands of mighty angels, all of them strong and regal in their appearance. Some had wings and others did not. They were neither male nor female. Some were mighty warriors with beautiful glowing skin and long flowing hair. Some were as much as twelve to fifteen feet in height. Others were not as tall but still exceptionally large and powerful. *So is this heaven?* he thought to himself. He looked at Arrikahn to see if he was going to answer his question without speaking it. Arrikahn looked down at Thomas with a sly grin on his face as if to indicate that he would only answer at the times of his choosing.

"They were floating above a bright golden path, with multitudes of people on either side standing at attention. Thomas noticed a look of pure joy on their faces. He could tell they were humans, yet their countenance glowed in a beautiful way in which Thomas had never seen. There were different terraced levels of the Great Hall; each level seemed to hold more importance than the last. Thomas then saw a door open and he heard a voice like the sound of a trumpet say, 'Come up here, and I will show you things which must soon take place.' Immediately he was in the Spirit and beheld a magnificent throne set in heaven at the highest level, which emanated a power that somehow was both the light and the life source of the great room.

"Just like in Scripture, Thomas saw twenty-four elders sitting upon twenty-four smaller thrones grouped in balconies around the main throne. The elders were clothed in white robes and they had crowns of gold on their heads. Before the great throne there was a crystal sea, and in the midst of the throne and around the throne were four living creatures full of eyes in the front and back. The first living creature was like a lion, the second living creature like a calf, the third living creature had a face like a man, and the fourth living creature was like a flying eagle. The four living creatures, each having six wings, were full of eyes around and within. They never rested but continually spoke the words, 'Holy, holy, holy, Lord God Almighty, who was and is and is to come!' Thomas noticed whenever the living creatures gave glory and honor and thanks, the twenty-four elders would fall down before the Lord and worship him, and cast their crowns before the throne, saying, 'You are worthy, O Lord, to receive glory and honor and power; for you created all things, and by your will they exist and were created.'

"In an instant, Thomas found himself thrust before the great throne, upon which sat the Great I Am, God the Father. Next to him sat King Jesus, whose appearance was like a magnificent crystal, glowing with the light of a jasper and a ruby stone within, and there was a rainbow around his throne, shining like an emerald. From the throne came forth lightning, thunder, and voices. Seven lamps of fire were burning before the throne. Feeling insignificant yet with nowhere to hide, as thousands upon thousands of the heavenly host surrounding him were looking on, Thomas stood alone before the awesome presence of the One True God. He knew of nothing else to do but fall to his knees and bow his head in reverence.

"As he trembled in fear with his eyes closed, he heard Arrikahn say to the Lord, 'Your Majesty—Justice Clarence Thomas, as you requested.' Thomas had been unaware of the beautiful music playing in the background, somehow surrounding them like an invisible heavenly fog. He became aware of it because it suddenly stopped. The magnificent hall was eerily quiet, except for the continuous reverent chants of 'Holy, Holy, Holy' from the twenty-four elders. The moments seemed like hours as Thomas debated within himself whether he should even look up. He finally gathered the courage to lift his head upward. He exerted all his strength but was unable to look upon the Lord, whose countenance brightly permeated Thomas's vision as he knelt trembling before the throne.

"The depth of Truth in the Lord's eyes, which burned with a holy fire, was more than Thomas could bear to look upon. Nothing that is, or ever was, could be hidden from him. The terrible power of his wrath was much greater than Thomas had ever imagined, as was the depth and warmth of his unconditional, merciful love, which Thomas felt penetrate to the very center of his soul.

"As Thomas knelt, trembling before the throne, the Lord said, 'Clarence Thomas, do you know who I am?'

"Thomas said, 'My Lord, you are the Christ, the living Son of God. In this moment of my passing, it is an honor to be in your presence, Lord. I beg for your mercy!'

"The Lord said, 'Your time has not yet come, but it is not far off. I Am as you say. I Am the Truth, yet you deny me. You deny me and yet you expect me not to deny you before my Father. Is that wise, my friend?'

"The Lord then spread his arms outward toward his great throne and said, 'I have brought you here to show you my throne. It is both my throne of grace, as well as my throne of judgment, but it is always my throne of truth. As you have read in my Word, mercy is greater than justice. Everyone must come through my throne room. Whether they receive mercy and grace or justice for their deeds is completely up to them. You have sat in judgment most of your life. You understand the responsibilities of the judge. You must have the wisdom to temper judgment with mercy. It is my desire that all receive my grace, which I have bestowed upon them. Grace is the only thing that will temper judgment.'

"The Lord stretched forth his hand toward Thomas, and immediately, as if his mind's eye had become a video screen, moments of Thomas's life flashed before him at the speed of thought. The Lord said, 'All men must give account for every word spoken and every action taken in the course of their lives.' King Jesus then pointed at the apostle Paul, who was seated in one of the smaller thrones to his right. He said, 'I visited Saul of Tarsus on the road to Damascus one day, just as I am visiting you today. I gave Saul the opportunity to receive grace, rather than just compensation for his deeds. I am doing the same for you today. In your earthly position of justice of the Supreme Court, you have been given the responsibility of ensuring a major piece of my plan for mankind is carried out in the form of jubilee on earth shortly before I return for my chosen beloved. So far, you have failed in that responsibility. Now is your chance to turn your failures into good works.'

"Thomas's thoughts immediately turned to his failure to ensure the Truth of the Supreme Court's ruling of the writ of mandamus was made manifest in the earth. Pictures of the entire story of Plan A appeared on the big screen: all of the orders given to the US Marshal's office for the arrests of the individuals who played a part in the cover-up; all of the private discussions held by the Supreme Court behind closed doors; and the court orders to turn the funds over to First Central Holding Company. The Lord said, 'Do you remember this moment?'—the moment in time when Thomas made the decision in private to allow the cover-up to continue and not seek the enforcement of the Supreme Court order. Thomas thought, *How was he able to pinpoint the exact thought I had?*

"The Lord answered him. 'You have read in my Word the proverb that states, "The eyes of the Lord are in every place, beholding the good and the evil." My Word is quick, powerful, and sharper than any two-edged sword, piercing even to the dividing asunder of soul and spirit and of the joints and marrow, and is a discerner of the thoughts and intents of the heart. My Spirit knows all the thoughts and the intents of the hearts of men. Nothing that is, can be hidden from me. By me and through me were all things created.'

"The Lord then looked upon Thomas with the deepest look of compassion, and said, 'My love for you is an everlasting love, just as is my love for all mankind. It is my desire that none should perish. The time is not far off when I shall return to the earth to retrieve my beloved. Many men allowed themselves to be deceived by lust for the temporary riches of the world in which you now live. You see, it is the love of money that is the root of all evil. Many you know have become a hindrance to the blessing of jubilee, which I desire for all men. However, those things which are bound will soon be set free. My purpose for what you refer to as "the First Central case" is Jubilee. Jubilee is more than just money; it is setting the captives free. It is a wave of my love sweeping the earth in the last days just before my return, so that all men may taste of my goodness.

"'Jubilee will represent to all mankind the freedom to taste of my mercy and see that it is good, before the judgment and the prophecy of the great end-time harvest may be fulfilled. I placed you in the position of responsibility for this specific purpose: it is within your power to remove this hindrance now restraining the blessing of Jubilee from touching all people. You must have courage and know my Spirit is with you, and you must know my mighty angels shall be there to protect you. Do not hold on to the fleeting security you now believe is important, for it too shall pass away. My Will shall be accomplished on the earth with or without you.

"'You must know your decision carries with it the blessings of life or the curses of death. The choice is yours. Fear not. Choose wisely. I cannot choose for you. But I would say unto you this day, choose life that you may reign with me for eternity! To whom much is given, much is required.

Meditate long and hard on your choices, for truly you will be held accountable. Again, know I love you enough that I took on flesh and walked among you. I know your feelings, I know your hurts, and I know your pains. I desire your presence amongst us for eternity. I will not fail you.'

"The Lord then paused as his everlasting love permeated the very space between each cell of Thomas's molecular structure, bringing with it an incredible peace the judge could not comprehend.

"King Jesus then said, 'I leave you with a final thought: you have tasted of my goodness; do not allow the cares of the world to consume you. The true, eternal world is the perspective you now hold. You now clearly understand the connection between your earthly choices and your eternal destiny. When you return to your earthly realm, my Spirit will speak to you and guide you. You are known in these halls as a mighty man of valor. May your heart continue to remain so. Choose well, my friend.'

"Thomas had been on his knees before the mighty throne of God, with his head bowed, as he listened to the powerful words of his Creator, when he suddenly became aware of the silence surrounding him. Not knowing what to do next, he looked up and was shocked at what he saw—the dark walls of his bedroom! He sat up in his bed, grabbing his covers to make sure they were real. He felt his forehead, realizing his face was covered in sweat. He was confused. The memory of his divine visitation was crystal clear, yet he was staring at his bedroom wall. Was it all a dream? Everything was so real—the details of heaven, the throne, the angels, and the words of the Lord. Was it a heavenly visitation? Did he really experience what he remembered, or was his mind playing tricks on him?

"Thomas quickly turned on his light and went into his study to write down everything he remembered from the dream, in as much detail as possible. His body was still trembling from vulnerably kneeling in front of the judgment seat of God. He made the decision, right then and there as he was writing, that nothing in this temporary life was worth experiencing the awesome wrath of God, as he had come face-to-face within his heavenly visitation.

"The Holy Spirit began to minister comfort to him as he was writing. A vision was revealed to him of a series of steps he needed to take to realize God's divine plan for his life. The more he wrote, the more inspired he became. His spirit began to break free inside. The chains of fear, which had him bound and powerless for many years to act according to what he knew to be right, were now falling freely, releasing their hold upon him. He had seen the Truth, and the Truth had set him free.

"From the moment the Freedom Central case had reached the Supreme Court in 1992, Thomas realized this was no ordinary case. He made a copy of every document that had reached the court: The history of the deal, the writ of mandamus; the court order to release the funds; the court orders of the warrants for arrest of the conspiring government officials, which were issued to the US Marshals but never enforced. All the information in the Treasury Department files regarding First Central Holding Company, Thomas had it all in a secret file, which he kept in the safe of his home. He had made a duplicate file and placed it in a safe deposit box. As he closed the safe, I instantly awakened."

*****

It was a bitterly cold Chicago afternoon. When an arctic front blows in from the north, with the driving wind from Lake Michigan in your face, walking the streets of the city is the last place anyone wants to be. Yet at two, the First Central brain trust was on the steps of Continental Illinois/ BankAmerica as scheduled. The anticipation was high. Everyone was excited. Could this finally be the moment they would have a breakthrough? What was beyond this moment? What doors would be opened? How would the American people react to the knowledge of the crimes of their government? Roger was preparing himself to give the most important speech of his life.

The problem was…*no one showed up!*

Not one person. They had received six verbal commitments from the follow-up of their pre-advice communiqués to the various media outlets. There were very few people on the street and not much traffic. They saw a television station news truck pass by the corner, slow down, and then speed off. That station was one of the six verbal commitments received. Possibly it was the weather, but probably, in retrospect, DeMarco Baily was informing his Illuminati higher-ups of every move Alex was making.

The orders then came down from the top that absolutely no one was to give an ounce of attention to the press conference. While appearing to assist in the organization of the event, DeMarco was in too deep as the double agent, having sold his soul for temporary gain long ago. When his superiors learned of the upcoming press conference, they squashed it through their far-reaching tentacles of power, letting it be known there would be serious repercussions for any individuals attending the press conference or reporting on it. Just one more example of the iron grip that the One-Worlders possessed on the media.

Having felt as if the winds were let out of their sails, they went inside the bank, requesting an audience, but were told no one was available to see them. Dejected but not defeated, they were resolute to pick up the pieces of their fractured plan. These men understood the law of perseverance. *Webster's Dictionary* defines the word *persevere* as follows: "to persist as in an undertaking; despite difficulties, to go on resolutely or stubbornly." These men had made a choice to walk by faith and not by sight. The circumstances did not dictate the reality of the situation. The spoken Word of God, full of life and power, was the master of the circumstances.

As depressing as the circumstances appeared, giving up was not an option. The only choice was to press on. As Captain Roger Golden continued to fight the good fight, he had no idea this would be his last stand. He was now only four months away from his appointment with his Creator. Roger crossed over without ever seeing his dream realized.

In George Orwell's classic futuristic novel *1984*, the powers that be were able to contort the perception of reality in the minds of the masses by controlling the vehicles and the avenues with which their messages were delivered. The hierarchy would simply "report" the information designed to have the desired effect on the people. The picture of reality placed into the minds of the masses would change to suit the needs of those in charge. America had become master of the distortion of Truth, squashing those in opposition to them in their battle to enslave the Truth in darkness. It is obvious the intended message to the public regarding the entire First Central story was that there was no story at all.

But that is simply not the Truth. Truth is a force beyond the control of mortal man. Truth chooses its own time and place to reveal itself. Darkness fears the light. The One-Worlders had built themselves a sandcastle for the entire world to see, built on a foundation of lies. One thing they did not count on was that high tide was coming, and the destruction of their fortress would be great! Soon, their sandcastle would be awash in the great Sea of Jubilee.

# The Magical Disappearance of the Federal Budget Deficit (or Not)

S aturday, June 21, 1997, the funeral procession made its way to the Barrancas National Cemetery at Pensacola Naval Air Station. Rows and rows of white tombstones flowed in orderly patterns across the gentle green hills of the landscape. The beautiful blue sky was ablaze on the hot summer afternoon. The Honor Guard, dressed in their sharp crisp navy-blue uniforms, did an outstanding job with their routine. The last words were pronounced over the casket of Roger Francis Golden, and the soldiers took their places for the traditional twenty-one-gun salute. A squadron of F-18s screamed overhead, tipping their wings to the deceased Naval Captain. The shots were fired as those in attendance absorbed the finality of the moment. The shells of the bullets were neatly folded inside the American flag and presented to the now-widowed Lorraine Golden, whose husband had passed away on Father's Day, June 15, 1997.

The family of Captain Golden walked away from the gravesite, not only devastated but experiencing an onslaught of emotions while searching for answers to so many unanswered questions. Roger was the captain of the family ship. They were sailing on a voyage together. They were supposed to arrive together; they were to do the Lord's work together, fulfilling their collective vision. However, it was not to be. Rich, the youngest son, remembered the words of his pastor, as he turned to look back one last time at the casket containing the body of his father. *When you think you've got it figured out, you know you've missed it.* Truer words were never spoken.

Alex was sensitive to Lorraine's situation and the void in her life. He made a conscious effort to keep her apprised of the latest developments. Lorraine had won over Alex's heart early on in their relationship by sending some of her delicious homemade banana nut bread to him on occasion. Alex was very gracious and appreciative to her, yet at the same time he would playfully flirt with her to keep the conversation light. Alex missed Roger very much as well, but he knew what he felt could not compare to how much Lorraine missed Roger.

Lorraine appreciated the void Alex was trying to fill and they became much closer over the next several months. She tried to be a good example for Roger and take notes of her conversations with Alex. Sometimes she would put dates on them and sometimes she forgot. She did not have a fancy notebook, but she did make the effort. She was worn out from the whole thing. But she knew Roger had put the last decade of his life into this deal and she wanted to respect his efforts and not let it die.

She told Rich in private that she wanted him to head up the family business and the affairs of Plan A. She also said she would do the communicating with Alex, who had told her he looked forward to their conversations. They were a refreshing change of pace from the daily burden of countless phone calls. The following are a series of notes Lorraine had taken from conversations with Alex:

*Note #1*
- Turnover package consisting of taxes, cash, assets, property
- Creating computer password for Alex
- Once tax treaty is executed, BankAmerica, Ill. Branch is ours
- Treasury Department: Mr. Holmes—contact
- Stock could tumble; might not be able to pay dividends
- We control ownership position and equity position

*Note #2*
- Questions being asked:
  - how to adjust bank stock?
  - what to do with problem banks?
- Cosmetics done, as per instructions from President Clinton
- I love you with all my heart! Your forever Frau!

*Note #3*
- Meeting called in bank this morning

- Plan on announcing new owner as of today (today through Wednesday)
- Great news: by Wednesday everything should be turned over to Mr. Gaus

*Note #4*

- Chief of Staff—Erskine Bowles now in charge of turnover
- Competitors out of it as of last night at 6:15, Friday
- Completed for turnover
- Wrangling with BankAmerica, Robert Coleman (VP of bank who gave Roger such a hard time)
- Watch for news Monday!

*Note #5*

- Mr. Erskine Bowles exiting next week
- Big splash—press release
- Call from D.C.—Bowles will finish, then resign
- Sen. Bill Bradley says, "Bowles is a straight shooter"
- Agreements ready for Gaus's signature, according to the way they agreed
- Taxes went up considerably—means more outstanding money was forced in
- Will Alex work from Continental Bank, controlling the other banks, or a central location?
- Response: "I own Continental Bank. I may as well work there!"

*Note #6*

- Treasury says, "All done." Official directly under Clinton
- Issuing Executive Order to turn this thing over
- For past five or six weeks, our deal has been completed. Top Washington lawyers trying to agree on procedures

*Note #7* (Howard Neece)
- Lot of activity between federal building and bank
- Bowles had to go back to Washington because of Chinese visit
- Bowles back in Chicago, at bank yesterday. This morning at fed building
- Bowles preparing documents for turnover
- Bank Trust debt secured by Secret Service
- Alex went back to the bank this afternoon—we are now waiting
- Final legal opinions approved by Clinton
- Bowles should give notification today or tomorrow to sit down with Alex for closing! Bank in Alex's name and First Central Holding Company

Someone once said insanity is doing the same thing over and over again and expecting different results. Maybe that was the case with the whole Plan A group. Continuing to believe the reports from the government, continuing to believe the fox when he says he will be exiting the chicken coop momentarily, the One-Worlders continued to pull the strings of government officials as if they were marionettes. The false messages of hope were passed on to Alex, continuing the pattern of the last ten years. DeMarco Baily, the man who sold out to darkness, continued until the last light left Alex's mind's eye. The eve prior to the supposed turnover, DeMarco confirmed to his superiors the presence of Alex at his residence. As Alex slept, ironically, he would take his last breath until the spirit within the humble warrior exited his earthly suit and his journey toward his eternal heavenly home began.

Alex Gaus, a mighty man of valor, crossed over to the other side to be with the Lord on June 2, 1998. Coincidentally (?), Alex's death was the same day he was scheduled to be in the bank for the official signings and closing procedures. The last flurry of communications was a final ploy to continue the deception being waged on Alex. The announcement of the surplus was a collective decision on behalf of the power players to provide a quick-fix catchall to the multitude of problems they had created for themselves. They could save face and keep the money they had stolen while sweeping all charges of wrongdoing under the rug and into the sea of forgetfulness.

Bank officials had offered the previous day to send Alex a limousine to pick him up and escort him to the closing at the bank, but being suspicious of their motives, he declined. He told them he would arrange for his own transportation to the bank. The next day—signing day—he was found dead in his bed. The One-Worlders ensured Alex died of *natural causes*. The infamous multibillion-dollar federal budget surplus speech was announced on September 27, 2000, by President Clinton.

The book of Hebrews describes a scene commonly referred to as "The Hall of Fame of Saints." The saints who have gone on before—everyone from Abraham to Zechariah—are gathered in heaven around a window from which they can see events on earth and cheer on their younger brothers and sisters: a great cloud of witnesses, if you will. Most assuredly, when Alex and Roger entered the gates of heaven wearing their well-earned garment of humility, they entered to a warm greeting from the saints. Not because they themselves were great but because of the desire of their hearts to see more of the attributes of Jesus and less of themselves; to see the fruits of the spirit manifested in their lives: love, joy, peace, patience, kindness, goodness, faithfulness, gentleness, and self-control; treating others the way they themselves would want to be treated; putting on the entire armor of God and standing on faith in the face of their evil enemy; with motives not based on greed and lust for power but on faithfully administering the assets of the Lord to the benefit of all mankind.

Truth knows the thoughts and the intents of the hearts of all men and women. This life is the equivalent of grade school, and people's thoughts, actions, and words make up their report card. The report card contains the data that determines their place in eternity, which people choose for themselves. Alex chose well.

Family members of Alex, consisting of sons and sisters, sent letters to BankAmerica and the Treasury Department informing them of the new board positions at First Central Holding Company. Their intent was to keep open the lines of communication with the government and bank officials. None of their communiqués received responses. The silence of the government officials clearly was a statement of their position: "Alex is dead, and there is nothing to stop us now."

After the announcement of the miraculous federal budget surplus by President Clinton near the end of his eight-year term as president, the first time in over sixty years that such an event has occurred, included in his speech was the commitment by both the executive branch and the legislative branch to pay down the federal debt with all of this newly found money. When the treasure chest was handed over to President George W. Bush, not one single penny of the federal debt was paid off as was promised. Within the first year of the Bush administration, the entire subject was quickly forgotten when the nation was paralyzed by the events of September 11, 2001.

There are many who debate the legitimate story presented to the people by the federal government regarding the events of 9/11. There are many reasons for that popular viewpoint; however, I will refrain from diving into that deep rabbit hole. I will, however, digress for a moment at this point to shed light on something I do not hear spoken of by the media nor by the prophets of God.

Chapter 18 of the book of Revelation is written as though the apostle John was shown a divine time machine and watched the twin towers burn and fall to the ground on the news media, just as did millions of people around the world. With the understanding that he was attempting to write what he saw with the verbiage and diction of two thousand years ago, here are some excerpts from his description. Three times in his description, he refers to the great city being taken down in one hour. "In one hour, thy judgment is come."

He refers to the great city as a queen sitting on her throne. We all can recall how majestic the twin towers stood above the rest of the great city as a queen sitting on her throne. He refers to the kings of the earth who have become rich over the merchandise of gold and silver, precious stones and pearls, fine linen and purple and silk and scarlet, and all manner of vessels most precious, wood and brass and iron and marble, and cinnamon and odors and ointments of frankincense, wine and oil and fine flour and wheat, beasts and sheep and horses and chariots and slaves and souls of men.

The merchants of these things, which were made rich by her, shall stand afar off for the fear of her torment, weeping and wailing. For in one hour so great riches is come to naught, and every shipmaster and all the company of ships and sailors and as many trade by sea stood afar off and cried when they saw the sky filled with the smoke of her burning, saying, "What city is like unto this great city?" They cast dust on their heads and cried, weeping and wailing, saying, "Alas that great city wherein we were made rich, all that had ships in the sea by reason of her costliness, for in one hour is she made desolate, as they stood and watched her smoke poured up into the sky."

We all can recall that each of the twin towers fell to the ground within one hour of the time that they were first hit by the initial projectile. New York City was certainly the greatest trading city in the history of the world, and the apostle John used many words of exotic things to try to explain how through the New York Stock Exchange and NASDAQ and other avenues of revenue exchange, that this was indeed the greatest trading city known to man.

Who can forget the people running around the city with the dust of the explosion covering their faces and heads, screaming in terror? The most important part of chapter 18 is found in verse 21, where it states, "And a mighty angel took up a stone like a great millstone and cast it into the sea, saying thus with violence shall that great city Babylon be thrown down and shall be found no more," and it continues to describe great destruction of the great city, with the final sentence of chapter 18 reading, "and in her was found the blood of prophets and of saints and of all that were slain upon the earth."

Is it a coincidence the events of 9/11 took place at the same time the federal debt was to be paid off? More importantly, in verse 21 of chapter 18, when the mighty angel picks up the giant millstone—or asteroid in modern terminology—and casts it into the sea, this represents judgment by God. This is a deliberate act by an angel who is under orders from the Most-High God. A mighty angel would not conduct such an act on his own but only upon orders from his commander. Certainly, God would not execute judgment without a great offense transpiring on planet Earth, causing his anger and wrath to rage. If such an offense did occur, the question could be asked: why was his judgment not executed sooner? My only answer is that God allowed a period of grace for men and women of the earth to repent and come to know King Jesus and get on board the heavenly train before it leaves the station. I am not saying it is or it isn't, but the scenario presented certainly is something to consider.

I am certainly not making light of events and the lives lost on 9/11. However, it is indisputable how uncanny are the similarities of the descriptions written by a man days away from his death, alone on a deserted island, describing the events of that tragic day with amazing accuracy.

Two more things to consider on the subject before moving on. Is it a coincidence that in the late nineties, two blockbuster movies came out at the same time with the storyline of an asteroid heading toward Earth? Most of you have seen these movies and are familiar with the storyline. Is it a coincidence that for the past twenty years, massive underground bases have been constructed with the intention, many believe, of allowing the few elite to survive such a disaster, with the magnitude of a giant millstone being cast into the sea and the aftereffects thereof?

Is it a coincidence that one of the first initiatives undertaken by President Trump upon assuming the Oval Office was the creation of Space Force, the newest branch of the American military? There are many who believe that, in the mid-'90s, NASA secretly discovered such an asteroid on course for Earth and kept it secret from the public to avoid mass hysteria. If such a discovery were true, it certainly could be a common denominator amongst these questions. The deep state enhancing the underground mountain bunkers to save the elite, and Space Force being created to attempt to destroy such an asteroid to save mankind.

There are many who debate the legitimate story presented to the American people about the motives behind the invasion of Iraq and how one subject relates to another. There are many who claim the real reason for American military forces in Iraq and Afghanistan had nothing to do with 9/11 or Saddam Hussein or weapons of mass destruction. It is interesting to note that during the reign of the Taliban regime in Afghanistan, the flow of opium from the Far East through the Middle East and into the secret processing plants of the One-Worlders on the Mediterranean coast of Monaco and France was at an all-time low. A little-known centuries-old legend is when the great sailing ships of Britain sailed to the Far East to obtain the exotic teas that were so valuable to the civilized world, what they had really done was create opium addicts out of the working-class people of the Far East. They then transported this product along with exotic teas to the western world and created an unprecedented cash flow, which went a long way to enhance the wealth of the few ruling-class families of the Illuminati.

This, allegedly, has been a cash flow of these elite families for centuries, passed down from one generation to the next. When the Taliban tried to shut down the opium flow, these ruling families would have none of it, and the order was sent out for the Taliban to be taken out. One fact that is overlooked from the presence of the American military in Afghanistan is that, once the Taliban was taken out of the picture, the flow of opium from the Far East through the Middle East to the processing plants on the Mediterranean coast reached an all-time high. This was the real game.

It is no coincidence the number of heroin overdoses in America increased to an unprecedented level during that time as well. There are no coincidences when it comes to the game plan of the One-Worlders. There was no reporting of this in the mainstream media. They were spoon-fed their information from the deep state and the hysteria of the war. Even the justification of why American military personnel were dying in Iraq and Afghanistan was all the American citizens heard and saw on the news.

One of the first acts signed into law when President Bush took office was that every single contract of any kind regarding the United States military was to be funneled through the Halliburton Corporation. Coincidentally, Vice President Dick Cheney was the former chairman of Halliburton but stepped down from his position to take the office of VP so there would be no conflict of interest (wink, wink, nod, nod). The amount of the American taxpayer's money spent on this war culminated in a $10.6 trillion federal debt at the end of the Bush administration in 2008.

The baton was handed off to the Obama administration. Fast-forward eight years later, and in 2016, at the end of his second term, the federal debt was now $18 trillion. Not one penny of the federal debt was paid down as was promised when President Clinton announced the federal budget surplus in the fall of 2000. The American economy is on the verge of collapse resulting from these irresponsible actions of American leaders at the highest level. Every senator, congressman, and the highest leaders of the Oval Office should face prison time for allowing the American economy to flow over the waterfall of disaster when they had every opportunity to eliminate the federal debt completely. Of course, that was not an option they would consider when their real motive was to intentionally destroy the American economy so it would be easily integrated into a One-World monetary system. As a result of this huge federal debt, the Federal Reserve was forced to print money out of thin air to keep the economy afloat, while they allowed China to buy federal notes and treasury bonds at an alarming rate.

This coincides with what has been discovered regarding the amount of military secrets and economic espionage that our leaders handed over to China for decades. Keep in mind, God's plan was decades ahead of the One-Worlders' plan. Remember in 1992, when the Supreme Court ruled in favor of the court order issued by Judge Gesell, when the original $1.7 trillion owed to first Central Holding Company became $7 trillion after three years, interest, penalties, and interest on penalties. Because of the bribes handed out by Alan Greenspan to everyone who was someone in Washington, that Supreme Court order was quietly tucked away and sealed in the Supreme Court vault.

However, Judge Gesell had set a precedent with his ruling when $1.7 trillion turned into $7 trillion over a three-year period. The most important part of the story is that the interest clock never stopped ticking. When the mathematical equation is extrapolated out with compound interest kicking in somewhere along the way, in the year 2020 the amount owed to first Central Holding Company, and vicariously to the American citizenry, is now over $528 trillion! That which is hidden in darkness shall be made manifest by the light.

One last item to consider before moving to the next chapter. It was with great sadness America read of the tragic death of Justice Anton Scalia on February 13, 2016. There are many who believe that his death, while tragic, poses more questions than answers. The deep state, many believe, had a sixteen-year plan in their execution of the realization of a one world government. President Obama was the first half, or, to put it in baseball terms, the setup pitcher, and Hillary Clinton was the closer. No one thought she would lose. With the understanding that Justice Scalia was the most vocal opponent of the unexecuted Supreme Court order cover-up of the 1990s and the Clinton administration, and the fact that he knew all the secrets hidden away and sealed in the Supreme Court vault, is it possible the timing of his death was more than coincidence?

That subject certainly has been a subject of debate since his death and can only be speculated upon. Clarence Thomas and Ruth Bader Ginsburg are the lone remaining Supreme Court justices who participated in the cover-up of the Supreme Court Order; however, Justice Thomas was silenced early in his career with the drama surrounding Anita Hill.

I would challenge him, after reading this book, as he was in alliance with Justice Scalia, to comment on his viewpoint of events surrounding the unexecuted Supreme Court order. With every photo of him on the bench, the look on his face is one of disgust, knowing that the integrity of the Supreme Court has been compromised for the entire duration of his tenure on the bench.

Remember, both Prophets Kim Clement and Mark Taylor are on record prophesying of a giant scandal that will rock the integrity of the Supreme Court bench. Could this be that of which they spoke? No one knows for sure yet, but it is certainly possible those things which have been hidden in darkness shall be made manifest by the light. Truth is a force beyond the control of mortal man.

# The Stimulus Trillions

The story of the hidden trillions of dollars owed to first Central Holding Company and thusly the American citizenry continues to the first term of the Trump administration. Donald Trump did not inherit his billion-dollar empire. He certainly was not raised in poverty, but he knows how to run a business and turn a profit. He may not have been well-liked as he built his empire, but at some point, he had a change of heart and became a humbled man of God who believed in the power of prayer. At some point, he had his own Damascus Road experience, just as Saul had when he became the apostle Paul. Perhaps it was because an elite group of military officers came to him and asked him to run for president in 2016. They cautioned that if he declined, they would exercise a military coup to avoid the intentional destruction of America by a group of global elitists.

A military coup is the last thing anyone wanted, so they requested Trump's assistance in saving America, through legal means. The deep state controls the mainstream media and they receive their talking points from the deep state sources themselves. This explains the constant negative press against this president. However, it has become evident that President Trump is God's man of the hour, full of faith and power, and there are many who believe in the power of prayer, both inside his administration and throughout the country. For example, is it a coincidence that numerous times throughout the book of Revelation the angel of the Lord is commanded to sound the trumpet, which essentially is the meaning of the name Trump, connected with the fact that according to biblical prophecy, it is widely believed we are living in the end times? There are many who would say it is beyond coincidence.

The deep state has made a constant effort since he was elected to take him down. First, it was Russian meddling in the elections. Then it was the Mueller report. Then it was the unsuccessful impeachment effort. While all of this was happening, the economy statistically became the best ever, with the stock market crossing over the 30,000 mark. Enter COVID-19 and the global economic shutdown.

At first glance, this would appear to be a deep state victory against President Trump, as the economic numbers started to crash. There are many who believe this was a cover-up of the most heinous crimes in history, the crime of human trafficking, which has become the most profitable act of crime in history. These crimes are being revealed under the Trump administration more than any administration in history by many times over. However, this global pandemic allowed him to declare a national state of emergency, and in so doing, he was able to move the unconstitutional Federal Reserve under the authority of the Treasury Department, eliminating the autonomous status of the Federal Reserve.

By placing the feds under the authority of the Treasury Department, the feds is also under the authority of the office of the president. This allowed him to put the microscope on the Federal Reserve, where he discovered the trillions of dollars hidden in the many financial tributaries of the Federal Reserve system. Alternatively stated, he discovered the funds accumulating in the name of First Central Holding Company.

He has been mysteriously passing out trillions of dollars to American citizens and small businesses throughout the country to keep businesses afloat and individuals from going broke. Many ask, where are these stimulus trillions coming from? But they do not spend too much time asking those questions, they merely stick their hand out, receive their portion, smile, and say thank you. The Federal Reserve has never been audited; however, many believe an audit will soon take place under the Trump administration. Along the way, a new gold standard economy and the trillions discovered in the upcoming audit of the Federal Reserve represent the beginning of a national and eventual global jubilee.

The purpose of this book serves as an impetus to the realization of financial jubilee. This book seeks not punitive action against any of the conspirators; those chips will fall where they may, and the perpetrators will stand before Truth at the appointed time and account for their actions. This book stands as the culmination of a twenty-five-year pursuit which began when the Holy Spirit spoke clearly into my spirit, *Jubilee, jubilee, jubilee!*

# The Federal Land Dispensation Act

King Jesus declared in the fourth chapter of Luke that he came to set the captives free—freedom for the captives in every area of life, including financial captivity, which is the basis upon which the Federal Reserve was founded and operates. The ability to enslave the masses into a system that operates on creating wealth out of thin air and then charging interest on the masses for the privilege of using the money they have created results in an endless spiral of debt, to which most Americans will remain captive.

The motive behind the Jubilee movement is to set the captives free financially from the enslavement to the world system. This is not about religion. Remember, religion is to visit the fatherless and widows in their affliction and to remain spotless from the world. This is about a philosophical system of finance that is contrary to the world system. Where the spirit of the Lord is, there is liberty. Remember, the first thing *Wikipedia* says about federal lands is that they are lands owned by the federal government. Who is the federal government? We the people, by the people, for the people. The federal government is not a club one must have certain credentials to join; the federal government is made up of millions of "we the people."

Earlier in the book, a plan was laid out for every voting American citizen to experience, through a specifically designed matrix of data, their individual pixel of the ownership of federal lands in a logical, tangible way. Every portion of the matrix would be backed by 100 percent collateral through their portion of the federal and state lands each citizen owns via the Jubilee Matrix. Those who choose to cash out will be funded through the Federal Reserve, and their share of land will serve as the collateral held by the feds, just as a piece of real estate fully owned by an American citizen could be mortgaged at 100 percent of the value and the title deed would be held by the funding bank.

What this means to every voting American citizen is that they can all cash out for a mortgaged value of $500,000 or retain the value of the real estate portion of the matrix with the expectation the value would increase.

America is divided and bleeding, and the declaration of the Federal Land Dispensation Act would go a long way toward healing those wounds and unifying our great land. All voting American citizens would be given an equal slice of the pie, which would set the captives free financially. There would be no reason to riot but rather rejoice! Those that are found guilty of rioting would lose their share of ownership, and their shares would be returned to the matrix. They would also undergo due process and face possible prison time.

Whether you are a Democrat, Republican, Independent, Libertarian, or some other party affiliation does not matter. All voting American citizens would be set free equally from the bondage of the world system. Those who yesterday felt like they had no future would soon see their future possibilities will be endless. Just as God's grace is given to all freely and equally, Jubilee sets all financial captives free financially as a symbol of God's unconditional love to all his children before the heavenly train leaves the station.

An American citizen does not have to have a relationship with their Creator to be set free financially through the Jubilee Land Plan. However, to not do so would be the greatest self-inflicted wound imaginable. There are no strings attached as God gave us all free will and the ability to decide. He does not want robots; he wants us to get to know him and love him because of how wonderful he is. The point being that every voting American citizen will be set free financially regardless of their relationship with their Creator.

The files of the Supreme Court for the week of October 5 through October 9, 1992, are requested to be unsealed. The Supreme Court order issued on Wednesday, October 7, 1992, was conducted en cameo, which is a term for sensitive, highly political issues that are discussed and voted on in a nonpublic forum. The release of these sealed documents and the execution of the original court order will result in the elimination of the federal debt and well over $1 million for every voting American citizen extracted from the Federal Reserve. From 1989 to 1992, the commissions owed to First Central Holding Company increased from $1.7 trillion to $7 trillion. Extrapolated out, the funds now owed to First Central Holding Company over thirty years is $528 trillion. Roger Golden, the late attorney representing the interest of First Central Holding Company, and the late owner thereof, Alex Gaus, have appointed to me, Rich Golden, power of attorney over these issues, and I hereby demand these funds currently held under the control of the Federal Reserve to be distributed to the American citizenry in an equal portion. The Treasury Department, and the Federal Reserve, which is now controlled by President Trump under the declaration of the national state of emergency, is thusly requested to audit the Federal Reserve relative to this information. This is a massive paradigm change of the people by the people and for the people. The $528 trillion will erase the Federal Debt, restore Social Security, and distribute the balance to the American citizenry, as well as becoming the active centerpiece of the Jubilee Matrix. Combined with the Jubilee Land Plan, $1.5 million is provided to every voting American citizen. Based on the crimes committed over decades, the Federal Reserve Bank is requested by the American Citizenry restructured to manage the Jubilee Matrix under the Department of Treasury, and the IRS to be disbanded for their crimes against the American citizenry with a flat sales tax replacing the current system. This is an act of liberation for those held in financial captivity across the land. This is truly Jubilee.

This is not about Republicans or Democrats. For decades, both parties have covered up the corruption at the highest levels of justice. When King Jesus announced his ministry to the world, declaring he came to set the captives free, this included liberating the captives spiritually, physically, emotionally, and financially. God is no respecter of persons, and the dispensation of Jubilee is freedom for all people, symbolic of God's unconditional love for all mankind. The wealth and freedom distributed through Jubilee are not for materialistic gain. Rather, it is sounding the trumpet of the nearing return of King Jesus to gather his people together in a great end-time harvest of souls before the spiritual train leaves the station.

My desire is that all who read this book would be on that train, but if only one person comes to know King Jesus because of Golden Jubilee, this will have been a worthwhile project. I pray peace and blessings upon all those who have read this book, and their eyes be enlightened to the power, grace, and majesty of our Creator.

# Epilogue

Write the vision and make it plain upon the tables
that he may run that readeth it. For the vision is yet
for an appointed time but at the end it shall speak,
and not lie: though it tarry, wait for it; because
it will surely come to pass, it will not tarry.

—Habakkuk 2:2–3 (KJV)

CPSIA information can be obtained
at www.ICGtesting.com
Printed in the USA
LVHW020222301121
704826LV00019B/321